Modern
Political Economy

Modern
Political
Economy

Bruno S. Frey

Martin Robertson

© Bruno S. Frey 1978

First published in 1978 by Martin Robertson & Company Ltd.,
108 Cowley Road, Oxford OX4 1JF

ISBN 0 85520 235 1

Phototypeset in V.I.P. Times by
Western Printing Services Ltd, Bristol
Printed and bound in Great Britain by Richard Clay Ltd, at
The Chaucer Press, Suffolk

Contents

vi   *Contents*

Preface

Political economy studies the interdependence between the economy and the polity of a country or countries. This book is entitled *Modern Political Economy*, because it refers to a *modern* society and uses *modern* theoretical and empirical methods. It is directed towards three types of readers.

(1) The *economist* is shown the importance of the state, interest groups and bureaucracy for an understanding of today's economy. The book thus is intended to help overcome the sterility of 'pure' economics.

(2) The political *scientist*, *sociologist* and *psychologist* are given an understanding of the theoretical and empirical approaches that derive mainly from economics.

(3) The *layman* is given an idea of the variety of scientific views and results, as well as of the main relationships between the economy and the polity.

Modern Political Economy differs in three respects from other works on the same topic.

(1) *Broadness of approach*. Political economy is not considered a closed theoretical subject; rather, the existence of various approaches serves to induce fruitful research. In particular, an attempt is made to combine *public choice* (which is heavily indebted to neoclassical economic theory) with the political economy of Unorthodox writers (such as Galbraith, Hirschmann and Myrdal), in order to reach a new political economy. This procedure mirrors my dissatisfaction with the presently dominating neoclassical theory as well as my intellectual bias for original ideas.

(2) *Empirical orientation*. In all variants of political economy the confrontation with reality as shown in statistical figures is grossly

neglected. It is shown in this book how the theoretical models can be empirically tested.

(3) *Simplicity*. What is important may be said simply. As political economy of Unorthodox writers (such as Galbraith, Hirschman simple terms. Thus there are no footnotes; the references to the literature are collected and commented upon at the end of each chapter.

Modern political economy is still in its infancy; it would therefore be a mistake to expect the same rigour as in long established fields. However, all shortcomings of content and presentation should be attributed to the author.

I am grateful to my collaborators, with whom I am united in the endeavour to create a modern political economy and who all have made contributions of their own. Jürgen Backhaus, Beat Ch. Blankart, Gebhard Kirchgässner, Werner W. Pommerehne and Friedrich Schneider have looked through first versions of the manuscript and have offered valuable suggestions for improvement.

Bruno S. Frey

Part I

WHY POLITICAL ECONOMY?

The economy and polity of a country are inseparably linked. Traditional economics however deals almost exclusively with the market economy, thus implying that economics may be separated from politics. Economics must become political economy in order for it to be able appropriately to grasp and influence reality – this is argued in Chapter 1. The analysis has to go beyond the price system and include other decision-making processes. Some of the most important social organising mechanisms are discussed in Chapter 2. The approach characterising modern political economy is illustrated in the third chapter, using as an example inflation and income distribution.

1. The Need for a New Approach

THE RELATIONSHIP BETWEEN ECONOMICS AND POLITICS

The economy and polity of a country are closely linked. Economic development depends on political factors, and economic factors have a strong influence on political decisions. Governments risk being thrown out of office if they fail to achieve a favourable state of the economy. They also may not undertake policies against major economic interest groups without risking unpleasant repercussions.

The mutual interdependence of economics and politics is world-wide and affects all political systems, and it has always existed. In the past decades, in which *government economic activity* has increased both absolutely and relative to the private economy, this interaction has become even more intensive. There is no sector of the economy that is not directly or indirectly influenced by the state. Representatives of big business have accordingly tried to affect political decisions in their favour. In some areas the distinction between the state and the economy has become untenable, particularly in areas dominated by public enterprises and with goods whose sale is guaranteed or actually undertaken by the state (as for example in the agrarian sector and in the defence and space industries).

The increasingly important role of the state in the economy is caused to a large extent by the demand of the population for goods and services that cannot be produced on the open market. The state is therefore given a role in the *allocation* of such goods. They are mostly '*public goods*', or those belonging to the infrastructure, such as education, basic research, defence, public transport and environmental protection.

In the open market, only those goods are produced for which a price can be asked from each single consumer of the particular product: those who do not pay may not consume. With public goods this condition does not hold; nobody can be excluded from consumption, even if he does not pay a price. For this reason, everybody tries to avoid paying a price, i.e. one tries to act as a 'free rider' in order to benefit from the payment of the others.

This characteristic of public goods may best be illustrated with an example from environmental protection. If the quality of air is improved by some measure, all inhabitants of the region concerned benefit from this improvement irrespective of whether they have paid a particular contribution. They do not pay a price specifically for the utility gained by the increased environmental quality. A private enterprise will therefore not supply such a good. For this reason, the supply of public goods and of the infrastructure belongs to the areas that are collectively organised. The citizens reveal their wishes for such goods and services in the political process of voting. Market forces and political allocation (in general) lead to different outcomes.

The financing of the production of the goods is also quite different. An individual payment for an individual good is substituted by general taxation. The means for supplying public goods is usually not by specific contributions, but through a system of direct and indirect taxes. These taxes are independent of the use of the public service financed. To state it differently, those who are particularly fond of clean air need not for that reason pay higher taxes. With the increasing importance of publicly supplied goods and services there is at the same time a separation between the *payment* and the *use* of production. This separation leads to a grave problem. It pays to ask for services from the state that will burden others with the resulting costs; or, conversely, it pays to try to achieve a reduction in taxes without having to sacrifice the consumption of publicly supplied goods. Though there is no possibility for society as a whole to supply public services without raising the necessary funds, owing to the separation of payment and usage each individual and each of the various groups has an incentive to secure an advantage at the cost of the whole community. The balancing of the public budget is therefore difficult to reach; a small number of political decision-makers is forced to consider jointly the income and expenditure side of the public accounts.

The increased importance of the state in economic matters is due also to the demands for an *equitable distribution of income.* In the past, as a consequence of rapid economic growth, aspects of income distribution took second place; it seemed more important that enough goods should be produced. With the achievement of a certain level of economic welfare, however, those groups that felt disadvantaged began to claim a 'fair' share of the national income. Today most people would agree that the state has a duty to guarantee a reasonable income to those members of society whose incomes are below a certain level.

In addition to the functions of allocation and distribution, there are many areas of economic activity in which the state intervenes, especially in the problem of controlling *business cycles*. With so much state intervention, one might suppose that full employment and price stability would be guaranteed. However, the state is not able to avoid inflation and unemployment; at times, it seems even to accentuate the disturbances by pursuing a pro-cyclical policy.

Economics and politics depend closely and intimately on one another in a modern society. Is this fact duly accounted for in current economic thought?

ECONOMICS AS THEORY OF MARKETS

Economics is mainly the science of the price system. It thus follows the tradition of Adam Smith and David Ricardo. In the centre is the proof of the optimality properties of a competitive market economy.

In the theory of the market it is shown that the private interests of individual suppliers, namely the maximisation of private advantage, leads at the same time to the maximisation of social welfare. The price mechanism has the particular property that it harmonises private and social advantage. This important idea of the classical economists is always in danger of being forgotten. It is, indeed, not always easy to understand. Proposals claiming to further social welfare in a *direct* way (e.g. by government regulation) appear to be more effective than the *indirect* way of using the price system. This common notion often turns out to be an error. There is little evidence for believing that the politicians and public bureaucrats involved in government intervention are interested in furthering abstract social welfare. It must rather be assumed that they are more interested in their own welfare. In contrast to the price system, other decision-making mechanisms do not usually harmonise private and social interests.

Economics has rightly turned its attention on the properties of the system of market competition. It has exactly studied under what circumstances the price system is able to so guide private interests that the result is advantageous for society as a whole. It has, in particular, been proved that, in the case of public goods, market supply is either impossible or does not function in a satisfactory way. The price system is able to bring about neither a just income distribution nor an automatic stabilisation of business cycles.

Present-day economics does not conern itself with the *political area*. The economy is thus treated as a unit isolated from the political process. Politics belongs to the 'institutional givens' which lie outside of the scope of the science of economics. However, this is only an outside appearance. When normative analyses are undertaken, an authoritarian political order is taken as a starting point: a 'benevolent dictator' or élite maximises 'social welfare'. The state is a godlike institution with complete information over all the wishes of the population, with no preferences of its own and always capable of achieving its will. The democratic process in which individuals can reveal their wishes by participating in politics is not considered. The pursuit of one's own interests, the fundamental principle of market behaviour, is negated in the political area. This constitutes a basic breakdown in methodology.

In other respects traditional economics restricts itself to a particular section of options available to individuals and groups. When changes in the conditions of economic activity (e.g. a raise in taxes) are analysed, current economics considers only individual adaptation in the market sphere (in the case mentioned, legal tax evasion and illegal fraud). In reality a great many reactions occur, for example the formation of interest groups, attempts to directly influence politicians, emigration to other communities or countries, and, of course, participation in voting and elections. Many statements made by traditional economists *appear* to be wrong to the public though they are – if applied to the market sphere only – quite correct. If the price of some good compared with other goods increases, for example, economic theory predicts a quantitative reduction in its consumption (at least if the income effects are negligible). But groups suffering from the price rises are often able to achieve a compensation from the state for (real or pretended) reasons of 'justice'. If such a compensation is granted, no reduction in consumption is to be expected, and no effective change in relative consumer prices has taken place. The prediction differs according to whether the purely economic or the whole politico-economic area is considered. The public and political planners are as a rule, however, interested only in the overall effect.

When such a disequilibrium arises (as e.g. the exogenously caused price increase), the difference between purely economic and overall effects may be substantial. In many cases a political reaction of those concerned may be less costly than an adaptation in the economic area. Under certain conditions therefore it is sensible to willingly create economic disequilibria, in order that these more effective political reactions will occur.

THE INEFFECTIVENESS OF ECONOMIC POLICY PROPOSALS

Economists are often unable to understand why their proposals for economic policy are mostly disregarded in political reality. They seem to feel that, once they have indicated the correct solution, all the politicians have to do is carry it out. If their advice is not followed, it is argued further, it is an indication of the incapacity or stupidity of politicians. They fail to see that the opposition of those who are adversely affected by these economically 'correct' proposals arises out of the same behavioural rationality that the same economists take for granted in the market sphere.

Those who expect to be disadvantaged by certain of the policies proposed are often capable of preventing their application by intelligent action in the political sphere. This may be possible if a well organised group (or one that can be organised because of the threat) is concerned or if those potentially to benefit are not very well organised. This is often the case when a limited number of persons or groups is *strongly* negatively affected, while the advantages of the economic policy measures are distributed thinly over a wide number of beneficiaries. Political action in this case is rational for the potentially disadvantaged, but not for the potential winners. Another method of political opposition is the coalition of those who are disadvantaged by a variety of economic policy measures.

Pareto-optimal solutions – where the utility of each individual can potentially be increased – may be subject to a similar fate. Economists as a rule do not consider it their task to determine the *actual* redistributions, which would in fact result in everyone benefiting by the proposal. It should not be overlooked that some groups may not be ready to support a proposal because *they* may benefit even *more* by a Pareto-inferior solution.

Economists engaged in practical economic policy often realise the ineffectiveness of solutions and proposals derived from traditional economic theory. They therefore endeavour to take account of the relationship between economics and politics. They generally consider these 'concessions to reality' to lie outside of their scientific competence, however. Because of their lack of education in this area, their thinking lies on the level of (enlightened) laymen.

The result is a separation of a 'pure' theory of textbooks from a 'practical' theory of political advising. 'Practical' theory cannot and does not meet the standards of science. 'Pure' theory, on the other hand, is considered unrealistic or even irrelevant by the public, because it is not ready to adopt the implied strict separation between the economy and the polity.

CONCLUSION

These reflections suggest that today's economists do not stand up to their tasks. Because of the failure to acknowledge the interdependence between the economy and the polity, reality is insufficiently explained and the economic policy proposals have little chance of being put into practice. A new orientation of economics is necessary. The *mutual relationships between polity, state and economy* must be put in the forefront. An economic science that does not account for political aspects is less satisfactory today than ever. Economics must be political economy.

2. Social Decision-making

Traditional economics is concerned almost exclusively with the functioning of the price system or the market. It was shown in the last chapter that this restriction has become very unrealistic; so long as it continues, economics runs the danger of excluding essential aspects of modern economy and of becoming irrelevant for many problems of today. Even 'purely' economic relations are not regulated solely by the price system. Conversely, the price system may be applied not only to 'economic' transactions in the sense of producing and distributing goods and services: prices may exist also for 'immaterial' goods.

The preoccupation of economics with the price system must be overcome, and a study of the many different reasons for taking a social decision must become part of economic theory.

The principles underlying social decision-making may be classified in various ways, each of them accentuating different aspects of the decision-making process. The classifications as such are without interest; what matters is that prices (or the market) is only *one* factor among a great many influencing a social decision even in 'purely' economic areas.

The simplest classification of these principles of social decision-making proceeds according to the number of components distinguished. In the *dual conception* the price system is confronted with an alternative decision-making mechanism. This implies a tendency to regard the alternative only as a negation of the market. A mechanism composed of three components evades this danger: the price system is seen as *one* among several factors of the same order designed to regulate social activities. The distinction of *four basic socioeconomic decision-making mechanisms* is particularly well suited for organised thinking and therewith, for analysis; the wide range of possibilities for social decision-making is acknowledged, but the number of components may still be grasped. One of the factors distinguished in this classification is, again, the price system.

The decision-making rules discussed below should be seen as abstractions and not as representations of reality. In the real world several systems co-exist; the analysis of their interactions is one of the topics of political economy. The knowledge of the functioning of each distinct type is, however, a prerequisite for understanding their interaction.

DUAL CONCEPTIONS OF SOCIAL DECISION-MAKING FACTORS

Market and plan

This traditional and often-used distinction is not fruitful but it is still the basis of many theories of economic policy and of the theory of economic systems. The opposing principles of decentralised and centralised steering of the economy are stressed. The dual distinction is insufficiently differentiated, however. Both types of steering may be undertaken in quite different ways. A plan may be established on the basis of democratic consent or bureaucratic orders (or by a combination of the two). The duality of market and plan also prevents the development of new conceptions, in particular when it is combined with the duality of capitalism and socialism: a planned economy is possible with capitalistic institutions of property (as for example in Nazi Germany), and socialism does not exclude market steering.

Market and voting

The market is often considered to be the 'economic' factor, and voting the 'political' mechanism, that serve to bring about social decisions. This confrontation is more useful than the one between market and plan because the *analytic* knowledge of the specific functioning of the two decision-making mechanisms is much better developed. It is well known, for example, under what conditions the price system and direct voting lead to a Pareto-optimal allocation of resources and where there is 'market failure' and 'voting failure', respectively. The dual view however lends itself easily to the mistaken conclusion that, implicitly or explicitly, allocation by voting is the only solution when 'market failure' exists.

Exit and voice

These two decision-making mechanisms describe the basic reaction possibilities facing individuals and groups when an institution (a supplier on a market, a public bureau, etc.) performs in an unsatisfactory way. In economics, the only option analysed is an exodus to competing suppliers. This forces the institution/firm concerned to improve its performance or to leave the market ('exit'). Political science, on the other hand, is more concerned with 'voice' or protest as a reaction mechanism. The leaders of the institution or firm are made to perform better owing to the protest raised by its members and customers; otherwise they run the risk of not being confirmed in their positions. Protest is also harmful for the private enterprise itself; the economic success of such a firm depends not only on its market activity but (sometimes even more) on the friendly terms it maintains with the civil service and the government. The protest of dissatisfied customers threatens the needed good relations with the political sector.

Exit and voice can be considered as either residual or alternative possibilities for action. Often, they are dependent on each other. The protest may not arise at all, or may have no chance of success, if the most active and most intelligent members and customers have turned to a competing institution. In economics, more attention should be payed to 'voice' as a decision-making category because of its increasing importance in some economic areas. Dissatisfaction with a product today often takes the form of protest because there is no corresponding substitute available (as in the case of monopolies or a public good, for example, or because there exists a sense of loyalty to a brand or a firm. Protest has been more and more institutionalised in the last few years. Private consumer advocates, in the style of the American Ralph Nader, or public institutions try to proffer consumers' wishes; and the press, radio and television devote increasing space and time to consumer protection.

Classification of only two decision-making mechanisms may be useful to subdivide the possibility set most easily and to call attention to contrasting properties. They may, however, describe the decision-making process in too simplified a way. If one of the two decision-making mechanisms does not function optimally we should not make the mistake of accepting the second factor as optimal without intensively studying its properties. All decision-making mechanisms are imperfect; it is, therefore, necessary carefully to analyse which mechanism is best suited for which problem.

A THREE-FACTOR THEORY OF SOCIAL DECISION-MAKING

Exchange, love and threat

This classification serves to stress that, in addition to the market, which is intimately connected with (voluntary) exchange, there are at least two additional decision-making mechanisms based on completely different ideas.

Love and affection, taken together as the *integrative system*, play their main role in the context of the family and small group. The integrative system works according to the formula, 'If I can do you good, I am glad'. An integrative relationship moves (consciously or unconsciously) away from the exchange system because this would destroy the foundations of the integrative system. Marital love for example would lose its meaning if it were considered solely from the standpoint of an economic cost–benefit analysis.

The decision-making mechanism of *threat* works according to the formula, 'If you don't do what I want, I shall punish you'. The threat system forms the basis of large areas of human behaviour. In modern industrial societies it is often used in the form of strikes or boycotts, for example. With respect to the relationships between nations it is particularly dominating. Compared with the exchange and integrative systems – which both tend to bring about Pareto-optimal improvements – the threat system has the unfortunate property of being likely to escalate. The use of threats often leads to a negative-sum game, in which *all* participants come off worse. This property has been confirmed by empirical studies on international boycotts.

The three decision-making mechanisms of exchange, love and threat appear rarely in pure form, but rather jointly, though with different weights. Even the market cannot function without mutual trust, i.e. without an element of the integrative system.

The integrative system has recently been introduced into neo-classical economics, though only in a curtailed form, while the threat system is still neglected. 'Pareto-optimal redistributions' are based on the idea of an individual having a utility function in which the welfare of another (or several other) individual(s) is included with a positive sign. A redistribution between these individuals (e.g. for philanthropic reasons) may thus be interpreted as an exchange benefiting both parties. This procedure is problematic; it contributes mainly to the formalisation but not to the explanation of observed phenomena.

Four Basic Socioeconomic Decision-making Mechanisms

Among the classifications with more than three components one has proved particularly useful. It differentiates between
- market or price system;
- democracy;
- hierarchy; and
- bargaining.

The price system and democracy are already included in the duality of market and voting. The other two mechanisms add important components of social decision-making. The mechanisms are now sketched in turn.

The price system

Market prices have the excellent property of steering the actor's self-interest in the direction of a maximisation of social welfare.

This harmony of interest between individuals and society applies only under very specific conditions, which frequently do not apply in modern industrial societies (e.g. the absence of externalities and of increasing returns to scale). It is moreover well known that the distribution of income and property resulting from the market is not 'just', and that a stability of prices and employment is not guaranteed. With respect to the allocation of the largest part of goods and services (at least for consumer goods above the subsistence level), the price system is far superior to other decision-making mechanisms because it functions automatically, without reference to centralised control, and takes account of consumers' preferences. In a planning system the quantification of the alternatives available must be imitated painfully and incompletely by a bureaucracy. The valuation of alternatives by the market holds, strictly speaking, only for those goods that are not affected by the conditions mentioned above. In the long run, and on the macroeconomic level, there are however externalities, as for example in the whole area of infrastructure; for many goods there is no valuation for the future, and in these cases the price system thus does not function.

Democracy

The properties of the democratic decision-making mechanism via voting are essentially known, though there may still be gaps in our knowledge.

There are a great many methods of determining the outcome of an election or vote. Best known is *simple majority*. Qualified majority (two-thirds, three-quarters) is used only when the *status quo* is especially to be protected. With the *plurality rule* the voters accord one point to the least preferred alternative, two points to the next lowest alternative, etc., and the alternative wins that has the largest total number of points. Instead of using fixed intervals for the valuation of alternatives, it can be left to the voter to distribute a fixed number of points (e.g. 10 points) over the set of alternatives. This is then called the *point rule*.

All these voting rules are subject to the danger of 'strategic' voting, i.e. that the individuals cast a vote that does not correspond to their true preferences. This possibility is especially present with point voting because the voters have the greatest options: there is a considerable incentive to accord *all* the points to the most preferred alternative in order to increase its winning chance. On the other hand, point voting gives the best possibility to indicate differences in preference intensity by the act of voting.

The rationality of social decision-making using a simple majority rule is called in question by the possibility of inconsistent results. As long as voting is confined to one dimension, e.g. the size of expenditures for a particular public good, there are few problems. As soon as the alternatives contain various dimensions (e.g. if a vote is to be cast on the size *and* the regional distribution of a public good), one has to reckon with inconsistent outcomes to voting. These problems appear not only with the majority principle but with *all* democratic decisions. They are the result of the fact that with all realistic voting rules it is necessary to choose between a *limited* number of alternatives and that no simultaneous comparison of the complete set of alternatives available is possible. As this restriction applies to plurality as well as to point voting, those rules are also subject to inconsistent results. The same applies to *representative political systems* with several parties and elections. (The questions concerning the problem of aggregation of individual preferences are dealt with more extensively in the second part of this book.)

Democratic decision-making systems can overcome some of the problems with which the price mechanism is confronted, in particular in the area of allocation of public goods (which are available to everybody) and goods with strong external effects. Elections and votes are often not applicable owing to practical reasons; e.g., they require too much time and material input. Moreover, in some cases the same problems occur as with the price system. Conflicts of distribution may be only very partially 'solved' by voting; and in the case of public goods that are subject to 'free rider' behaviour in the price system, the corresponding problem appears in the form of strategic voting.

Hierarchy

The hierarchical decision-making system is primarily found in bureaucratic organisations, which today play an important role not only in the government sector but also in large private enterprises. Hierarchy is defined by formalised chains of command from the top to the bottom, a pyramidal structure and vertical specialisation.

As to the decision-making mechanism, bureaucracy is in the offensive; it is indeed difficult to envisage how many decisions could be taken in another way in modern society. Traffic regulations on an intersection are best made by hierarchical decision (by police officers or through traffic lights) – the use of the price system (bids) or votes among car drivers interested in crossing would be quite ridiculous.

The hierarchical mechanism has obvious disadvantages: insufficient efficiency (by losing sight of the real goals and unnecessarily

high costs); slowness and the tendency to evade decisions and to
pass them on to other bureaus and levels; inflexibility and general
procedures which take insufficient account of individual cases;
lack of initiative; a strong tendency to push for the growth of one's
own institution and artificially to create new tasks. (All this has
been excellently described by Parkinson.) Bureaucratic decisions
are, moreover, not *a priori* more 'just' than, say, those of the
market.

Bargaining

This form of decision-making is prevalent in all those areas of
economy in which there is no strong competition. Bargaining is
prevalent between employers and workers, but it is also important
between oligopolistic suppliers and demanders, and when the state
acts as buyer in a specialised market (such as in the armaments
industry). With the attempts to establish an 'incomes policy', also, a
form of the bargaining system is used.

The properties of the bargaining system are relatively unknown.
Game theory especially created for that purpose has yielded some
insights that are of direct use only for the evaluation of this
decision-making mechanism. This failure should be attributed not
so much to game theory; it rather indicates the fact that a general
analysis of bargaining leaves open a large number of outcomes.
Only a detailed knowledge of the special conditions, i.e. theoretically based case studies, enable us sufficiently to restrict the set of
outcomes.

Within the bargaining system *logrolling* plays an important role.
Minorities can form coalitions, helping them to assemble a majority
for those issues that are of particular importance to them. A per-
manent exploitation of minorities by the majority is prevented in
this way; on the other hand, it is possible that special interests profit
again and again at the expense of the majority of voters and taxpayers, and that public expenditures are increased too far. The
unequal chance of forming interest groups is an important aspect of
the bargaining system. In general, producer interests (composed of
employers and employees) are easier to organise than the scattered
interests of consumers and taxpayers.

OTHER SOCIAL DECISION-MAKING MECHANISMS

Besides the mechanisms mentioned so far there are several other factors influencing social decisions. Here it is sufficient to mention *tradition*, i.e. decisions made according to proved standards of the past, and *chance*. The good properties of decisions via the principle of statistical chance are increasingly recognised in social science, but laymen find them difficult to understand. A proposition that is at least open for discussion is that of choosing Members of Parliament by chance because in this way each group in the population would be *really* represented according to its share in the population, and the result would be independent of differences in vote participation. This selection mechanism would, however, have disadvantages in other respects; e.g. it must be expected that members thus selected would be less competent and motivated than under the present system.

CRITERIA FOR EVALUATING THE DECISION-MAKING MECHANISMS

The properties of the various decision-making mechanisms can best be surveyed with the help of a *goal achievement matrix*. Such a matrix evaluates to what extent each decision-making system meets the criteria deemed necessary. Relevant criteria may be the classical areas of allocative efficiency, distributional justice (according to persons, groups, regions), stabilisation and economic growth. Moreover, the speed of decision-making and the cost of applying a particular decision-making mechanism (transaction costs) may be of interest. Number, specification and weight of the criteria introduced depend on the particular goal of the analysis.

Table 2.1 gives the goal achievement matrix for the case of the four basic socioeconomic decision-making mechanisms. A verbal or even numerical identification as to how far each decision-making system fulfils the various criteria would require a much more exact definition of the decision-making principles, going beyond the scope of this chapter. For the same reason the criteria are not weighted according to their relative importance, and thus no aggregation leading to an overall evaluation is provided here.

The goal achievement matrix is useful for understanding and

TABLE 2.1 *A goal achievement matrix for social decision-making mechanisms*

Decision-making mechanism	Criteria							
	Allocation	Distribution according to:			Stabilisation	Economic growth	Speed of decision	Transaction cost
		Persons	Groups	Regions				
Price system								
Democracy								
Hierarchy								
Bargaining								

evaluating social decision-making mechanisms even if it is not filled up numerically. The matrix forces us to look at each decision-making mechanism according to the same criteria in a coherent way, and thereby helps us to grasp its functioning. The special properties of the 'pure' mechanisms can better be judged by such a confrontation, and the *combination* of decision-making mechanisms appropriate for the problem at hand can be found. Not only bureaucratic units but also society as a whole is confronted with this task. The realisation of such new combinations of decision-making mechanisms often requires social innovations in order to create institutional prerequisites.

CONSTITUTIONAL CONTRACTS

The derivation of the goal achievement matrix described has advantages but also bears some dangers. It can easily degenerate into an exercise in classification without any analysis. The following objection is more fundamental. The criteria for the judgement of the decision-making mechanisms, and in particular their weighting, imply a social welfare function. The search for the best combination among the 'pure' decision-making systems constitutes the maximisation of a social goal function. However, only a dictator can maximise a social goal function. This approach of a 'benevolent dictator' contradicts – as already mentioned – the individualistic elements of a democratic society. It is necessary to analyse the process by which individuals come to a consensus about what social decision-making factors should be used. Only then is it possible to act collectively.

The following intellectual construction provides a solution to the problem. The individuals make a *contract* in the 'natural state', in which they have no information about their own future economic position and about their preferences. This construction allows them to keep the utility-maximising individual as the basic decision-maker, but forces them to look at the advantages and disadvantages of the particular decision-making systems in an objective way. This contract stipulates which decision-making mechanism should be used for the collectively organised activities. The individuals must moreover come to a consensus about what majorities should be used in the future for democratic decisions. The contract that regulates the basic elements of social decision-making, and may therefore be called a *constitution*, is voluntary. It thus materialises only if it is accepted by unanimous consent.

The approach of a constitutional contract uses a perspective different from the one used when establishing a social goal achievement matrix. The evaluation of the various decision-making systems for solving (unknown) future social problems is undertaken exclusively from the (representative) *individual's* point of view. He considers which decision-making mechanism and which voting rule are likely to yield him the greatest benefit. A goal achievement matrix may be useful for that purpose, in so far as it provides him with better information about the functioning of the decision-making systems. The principle underlying the constitutional contract is *procedural*: good is what is decided on the basis of correct procedures. What matters is not the particular outcomes of the application of social decision-making principles, but the use of the decision-making mechanisms that have been chosen for that purpose in the natural state.

LITERATURE

The notions of exit and voice as decision-making mechanisms have been developed by
> Albert O. Hirschman, *Exit, Voice and Loyalty: Responses to Decline in Firms, Organizations and States*. Harvard University Press, Cambridge, Mass., 1970.

The classification of exchange, love and threat has been introduced and analysed in a most original way by
> Kenneth E. Boulding, *Beyond Economics*. University of Michigan Press, Ann Arbor, 1968, and *Economics as a Science*. McGraw Hill, New York, 1970.

A book concerned more exclusively with transfer economics is
> Kenneth E. Boulding and Martin Pfaff (eds), *Redistribution to the Rich and the Poor*. Belmont, Wadsworth, 1972.

The analysis of Pareto-optimal redistribution goes back to
> Harold H. Hochman and J. D. Rogers, 'Pareto-optimal Redistribution'. *American Economic Review*, 59 (1969).

The best analysis and interpretation of the four basic socioeconomic decision-making mechanisms of market, democracy, hierarchy and bargaining can still be found in

Robert A. Dahl and Charles L. Lindblom, *Politics, Economics and Welfare.* Harper, New York, 1953.

A superb analysis of the properties of the price system is

Kenneth J. Arrow, 'The Organization of Economic Activity: Issues Pertinent to the Choice of Market Versus Non-market Allocation'. In R. H. Haveman and I. Margolis (eds), *Public Expenditures and Policy Analysis.* Markham, Chicago, 1970.

In particular, Arrow points out the need of mutual trust as a precondition for the functioning of the market.

The decision-making mechanisms are more fully discussed in the second part of this book, where also references to the literature are given. It suffices to mention one textbook in public finance which deals with the various types of voting rules (plurality, point voting, etc.):

Richard A. Musgrave and Peggy B. Musgrave, *Public Finance in Theory and Practice.* McGraw Hill, New York/London, 1973.

The funniest account of bureaucracy, which should, however, be taken seriously in many respects, is

C. Northcote Parkinson, *Parkinson's Law or the Pursuit of Progress*, John Murray, London, 1975.

A distinctive exponent of the idea of a constitutional contract is

James M. Buchanan, 'A Contractarian Paradigm for Applying Economic Theory'. *American Economic Review*, Papers and Proceedings, 65 (1975).

A survey and critique of this approach based on the works of John Rawls, Robert Nozick and James Buchanan is given by

Scott Gordon, 'The New Contractarians'. *Journal of Political Economy*, 84 (1976).

3. Inflation and Income Distribution

The specific properties and the usefulness of an approach can best be demonstrated by a practical application. A relatively new field such as political economy should not only be fruitful for theory but should also deepen the understanding of social processes and should thereby provide the foundations for successful political action.

The areas of application chosen are two macroeconomic problems of first-rate importance: inflation, and income distribution. Since World War II the general level of prices has continually been increasing in all developed industrial nations (to which this analysis is restricted). The problem of rising prices serves as a good example for application because there is a glaring discrepancy between economic theory, which has suggested effective measures to fight inflation, and economic reality, which reveals that the increase in the general level of prices continues unabated, and in many countries is considered one of the main economic problems, particularly since it is accompanied by considerable unemployment.

Income distribution is chosen as the second area of application because it serves to demonstrate that political economy can make a contribution to a problem that is of importance in practical economic policy but is disregarded in traditional economic theory. This applies particularly to the distribution of income between economic sectors and occupational groups.

This chapter is intended as an introduction to the *way of thinking* in modern political economy. The discussion touches on many elements that are treated more thoroughly in later chapters of this book.

INFLATION

Methods of fighting inflation

Economic theory contains many different approaches to and instruments for combating inflation. The various schools of thought differ, but they agree that price increases are not given by nature. From the purely economic point of view, inflation may be prevented. The following approaches may be distinguished.

(1) Inflation may be eliminated by creating a sufficient amount of *unemployment*. The argument is based on the Phillips relation according to which wage and price increases are negatively connected with the rate of unemployment. The increase in unemployment required to reduce price increases can be effected by an appropriate deflationary fiscal policy, i.e. by raising taxes and/or lowering public expenditure. The decline in the inflation rate is due to a dampening of trade union demands and to a downward revision of wage expectations of job-searchers.

(2) Inflation may be prevented by *controlling* the stock of *money*, a possibility stressed by monetarists. According to this view, the total volume of money may be steered by way of the monetary base (i.e. the sum total of currency with commercial banks and the public and the cash holdings of commercial banks with the central bank), for which the central bank is responsible. A reduction in the rate of inflation with a constant stock of money is attributed to adjustments in the form of wealth holdings of individuals and firms affecting goods and factor markets.

(3) Inflation may be fought by an *incomes policy*. Price increases are seen as a reflection of excessive claims on national income by the various groups in society. Incomes should be fixed *before* they are paid out in such a way that the real national income disposable is not exceeded. Practical instruments are moral suasion, social contract (in the United Kingdom) or 'concerted action' (in the Federal Republic of Germany). The same goal is intended with a *savings policy*. Its aim is to spend a smaller share of income received on consumer goods and thus to prevent the amount saved from entering the circular flow of income again. This requires an increase of the savings rate out of income. A successful savings policy has the advantage that it can both guarantee price stability *and* improve the distribution of income and property.

All these approaches agree on one point. If one country, in comparison with its main trading partners, has a lower rate of inflation, and if, therefore, its exports increase, import prices rise, and the stock of money is increased in order to keep the rate of exchange constant, every internal anti-inflationary policy will prove to be a failure. A successful internal policy to fight inflation must be accompanied by freely fluctuating or at least flexible exchange rates. This condition is, however, only necessary and not sufficient: even if the external sources of inflation are eliminated, the internal ones may continue and may possibly even become stronger.

In view of the fact that there is more than one method of fighting inflation, one wonders why inflation persists. There are two reasons: either the instruments of anti-inflationary policy are ineffective, or they are used not at all or only inadequately. In the first case the problem lies in the inadequacy of the policy; in the second case in the failure to apply it.

Ineffective policies

This problem applies particularly to *incomes policy*. It depends upon a voluntary and preceding determination of the incomes shares of the main social groups.

Even if a consensus is reached – which is not always the case – price stability is not guaranteed because there are many ways of getting around the agreements in a more or less concealed way. If labour is scarce, for example, the increase of the wage rate above the sum agreed upon may be in the interest of both employees and individual employers.

The decisive reason why a voluntary incomes policy as well as an authoritatively fixed incomes ceiling is never completely – and sometimes even most unsatisfactorily – followed in reality is that price stability is a *public good*. As 'non-payers' may not be excluded (each one is affected by changes in the general price level), it is rational for each single group to deviate from the agreements designed to secure price stability in order to reap the advantages of a stable price level without sacrificing income increases for its own members. Such a behaviour yields two advantages. A higher increase in nominal income is secured compared with other groups, and at the same time there are the advantages of price stability. If all groups use such reasoning, they all will have an incentive to deviate from the agreement. The incomes policy thus becomes ineffective. Every such policy breaks down when the participating groups are asked to renounce income increases which could be attainable according to market conditions. Interpreting price stability as a public good makes it possible to provide a reasonable explanation for the seemingly paradoxical fact that (almost) all people and groups declare themselves for price stability and join in an incomes policy, but that the guidelines and formal agreements are rarely complied with.

The failure should not be sought primarily with the persons involved in the negotiations. Often they are quite willing to keep the agreements, but they are not supported by their own group because from their point of view it involves a renunciation of a possible increase in real income. Such a sacrifice may be expected only if the leaders can decide authoritatively, a situation impracticable in a democracy. In groups with democratic structure self-interest usually prevails directly or is achieved by way of threatening, or actually carrying out, illegal strikes.

For similar reasons there are problems with *savings policy*. Two types of 'goods' should be distinguished here:

(1) a 'private good', in the form of accumulated savings accruing to those who participate in the savings policy, only; and

(2) a 'public good', in the form of price stability accruing to *all*.

As the private good is of quantitative importance in the long run only, savings policy is also confronted with the free rider problem: the person who does not increase his savings rate but rather consumes as much as possible is able to appropriate a larger share of consumer goods because the prices of these goods fall (relatively) owing to the higher savings of the groups joining in the savings policy.

Even if the chance of success of a savings policy is somewhat better than with an incomes policy, it is quite insignificant. Still, this instrument constitutes a step in the right direction because it is understood that, without a massive use of force or a sacrifice of the democratic structure of society, success is possible only if 'public' and 'private' goods are supplied *jointly*.

Failure to apply the instruments

The extent to which available instruments are used to combat inflation is determined by the interplay of political forces. In the centre are the government, interest groups and the central bank. Their behaviour to a large extent decides whether effective action is undertaken to fight inflation.

Government

In a democracy in which parties compete for power, a government has to follow voters' preferences in order to survive. The government's attitude *vis-à-vis* inflation is determined by the relative evaluation of this goal by the electorate. The party in power must try to calculate how much additional unemployment and how much of a drop in real disposable income voters are ready to tolerate for a reduction of the rate of inflation by 1 per cent. Empirical analyses (presented in Chapter 11 below) suggest that voters are unwilling to accept major unemployment in exchange for a reduction in inflation which is felt only in the future and which, possibly, is quite small. If this model of political competition captures reality reasonably well, each society has that rate of inflation that it desires.

Government depends, however, on voters' preferences only at election time; between elections it can afford to undertake political actions not necessarily popular with the voters. This discretionary freedom is used by politicians in power to secure their re-election. Instruments of economic policy are applied to bring about economic conditions especially favourable in view of a forthcoming election. For this purpose it may be particularly advantageous to pursue a restrictive policy in the first part of a term of government in order to dampen inflation. In the second part an expansionary policy may be undertaken so that a low unemployment rate and high growth of income are achieved by election time. The expansionary policy leads to an increase in inflation rates only after a time lag – i.e. after the election. The instruments to steer inflation are applied in the process of producing such 'political business cycles' (they are more fully discussed in Chapters 11 and 12), but they are not used throughout to combat inflation. It is an open question whether the average rate of inflation taken over the cycle as a whole is larger or smaller than if these instruments had not been used at all.

Interest groups

There are various avenues of influence in the political sphere, but it is particularly important to take account of interest groups. Their influence depends on many different factors. What matters most in this context are the different degrees to which latent groups may be organised. Interests do not unite spontaneously. An identity of goals is not sufficient to form a stable organisation because as a rule the supply of such 'goods' is intended from which supply exclusion is impossible. As this applies fully to price stability, only a few individuals can be expected to join an interest group whose goal it is to reach price stability and who will be ready to bear (significant) costs to finance its activity. This explains why there is no interest group of real importance fighting for price stability (and for other such general consumer interests).

The situation of *producers* is quite different. They have a political weight far exceeding their number. A government is able to win votes (or at least to stabilise its share of votes) by granting particular producers an increase in the price of their products; they experience a marked increase in income while the cost, in the form of a small rise in the general price level, is distributed over a large number of consumers. Under normal circumstances these price increases are not felt, except when they affect goods of central concern by tradition, such as milk and bread. A government is also able to win votes by helping specific groups of workers to increase their wages because the (probably) resulting price increase has a minor effect – only on consumers' budgets – leading at best to a small vote loss for the government on that account.

Consumers (as an entity) are also suppliers of labour ('producers'), and thus are both benefited and damaged by the government's actions. Within the family the wife is often a consumer exclusively (in the sense of not working in the open market). She is more affected by inflation than her husband because the household budget is usually adjusted to inflation only after a time lag. This explains why women have a stronger preference for parties in whose programme the fight for price stability plays a major role.

The greater influence of producers compared with consumers is especially obvious when a change in the rate of exchange as an anti-inflationary measure is considered. Revaluations are against the interests of export industry. Almost the whole country then considers itself to be a 'producer'; coalitions between employers and employees may indeed often be observed particularly in the export sector. The interests of the owners of capital and employees in this sector are directly affected by a cost increase of their product in the foreign market, and employment is endangered. Consumers, on the other hand, have difficulties in realising the beneficial effects of a revaluation because the reaction on prices takes a long time (up to two years). The government is confronted with a well organised lobby of export interests whose opposition may result in a loss of votes and possibly even in an election defeat. It can undertake a revaluation only if the voters positively value the use of instruments to fight inflation and react sensitively to any decrease in the rate of inflation.

Central bank

The central bank is generally taken to be the main defender of price stability. In many countries the central bank has a position independent of government and parliament because it is thought that the government, for political reasons, is unable to guarantee price stability. The question is, however, whether the central bank really wants to stabilise the price level.

The central bank should not be considered an abstract entity which in some way or other fulfils the 'will of society'. It rather is a *bureaucracy*, the members of which seek to reach goals that do not necessarily correspond with those of society as a whole. Their main goals are the increase in prestige, and self-preservation. Prestige is determined by the central bank's position compared with other bureaucracies (in particular the ministry of finance) and by the esteem it enjoys with its main 'customers', the commercial banks. Self-preservation consists of the will to survive and the autonomy that is maintained by minimising conflicts, especially with respect to the government. Regarding this, public opinion is of little consequence to the central bank.

The special relationship between the central bank and the government is most apparent in the reaction of the bank to wage claims that are considered a threat to price stability. The private sector could be forced to renounce price increases if the central bank were to keep the stock of money constant. This, however, requires a lengthy process of adaptation, leading to an unpredictable degree of transitory unemployment and to bankruptcy of some business enterprises. This cannot be tolerated by the government – especially not before elections – and so the central bank has to expand the supply of money.

A restriction of central bank policy to the control of the money supply, as suggested by monetarists, is in contradiction to the goals of central bank bureaucracy. The implied loss of function would surely lead to a loss of prestige; the central bank would probably not survive in its present form because an institution of lesser importance could take over this (at least seemingly) simple task.

For promoting its goals the central bank is interested in instruments that

(1) are immune against critique, i.e. may not be scrutinised by outsiders, owing to lack of information;
(2) open the possibility for overstressing successes and hiding failures; and finally
(3) leave greater scope for discretionary action.

For these reasons, the most suitable instruments from the central bankers' point of view are the numerous variants of 'moral suasion' as well as administrative interventions in the money and capital markets. These instruments are, however, of little effect for fighting inflation.

In contrast with the government, the central bank attributes more importance to the goal of price stability. Its main responsibility is considered to lie in this area, and accordingly it must expect to be attacked more severely when the inflation rate rises; whereas the responsibility for full employment falls on the government at least as much if not more than on the central bank. Indeed, empirical research has shown that central banks are ready to tolerate a great amount of additional unemployment for even a small drop in the rate of inflation.

Political economy and inflation

Political economy considers inflation and anti-inflationary policies to be the result of the interaction of economic and political forces. It does not restrict itself to the discussion of economic variables, as does traditional economics, but also endeavours to analyse the determinants of these variables. Its analysis does not stop with the question of whether inflation can *mechanically* be fought with the help of incomes, fiscal or monetary policies (*provided* the respective instruments are actually used). Political economy focuses on those economic and political forces appearing with *any* measure of anti-inflationary policy irrespective of the point at which the policy is applied and of how the policy adopted affects the price level.

INCOME DISTRIBUTION BETWEEN ECONOMIC SECTORS AND OCCUPATIONS

In a democracy with sufficient competition between political parties, the government is forced to take account of voters' preferences in order to be re-elected. In some countries (as in Switzerland and the United States) voters have a predilection for certain economic sectors, in particular for *agriculture*. A policy favourable to farmers rewards the government twice, since it satisfies the 'producers' in agriculture and also the city-dwellers. However, when the subsidies to agriculture get too large, the city-dwellers might have to pay too high a price for their predilection for agriculture, in which case they might withdraw their support for the government. The government uses a specific set of instruments to get around this conflict:

(1) the cost of subsidies is distributed among a large number of citizens so that they are little felt;
(2) the subsidies are made so complicated that it is practically impossible to find out what burden the rest of society really has to carry.

Import restrictions, which serve to keep up domestic agricultural income, contribute to inflation, but the consumers are unaware of what prices they would pay if agricultural products were freely imported. The same applies to price subsidies, which must be carried by the rest of society in the form of increases in direct or indirect taxes. Direct transfers are, on the other hand, unfavourable for the agricultural sector because the total amount of aid is relatively easy to determine.

Over-representation in Parliament

Under the majority voting rule, some economic sectors are more strongly represented in Parliament than they should be according to their proportion of the population. They are thereby able to secure higher incomes than would otherwise be possible. An important reason for parliamentary over-representation is the combination of

(1) the regional distribution of members of the economic sectors; and (2) the number and arrangement of voting districts.

The influence of these two factors may be illustrated in the following way. If there exists only one voting district, a group requires 51 per cent of the vote in order to attain an absolute majority. With three districts, only 33 per cent of the total vote is required, because a bare majority (i.e. 51 per cent) in two of the three districts is sufficient to gain overall majority. With five districts a 51 per cent majority in *three* districts is required, so an overall majority can thus be reached with something more than 30 per cent of the total vote. With twenty-five districts the vote share required to gain overall majority reduces to about 26 per cent of the total vote, and so on.

A group relatively unimportant numerically may therefore win if it gets a bare majority in just over half the voting districts. This extreme situation does not exist in reality. The farmers probably come nearest to fulfilling the conditions. In many countries there is quite a number of districts in which the agricultural interests are able to just mobilise a majority under present conditions, so that the farmers are over-represented in Parliament compared with their share in the population.

For quite different reasons the *civil servants* take many more seats in Parliament than corresponds to their share of the population. In the Federal Republic of Germany for example, 37 per cent of the delegates in the Bundestag are civil servants. In the Parliaments of the Länder the respective share extends from 28 per cent in Hamburg to 61 per cent in Hessen (1975). The reason lies in the most favourable relationship between benefits and costs of parliamentary activity for civil servants. Members of most other occupational groups – in particular the self-employed professional – suffer a considerable reduction in income when undertaking a political career. Civil servants on the other hand do not have any *private* costs of parliamentary activity. In many countries (e.g. in Germany) they are released from their official work but still receive their salary. While in Parliament they may even participate in routine promotions. The costs of political activity are in this case borne by all the taxpayers.

The strong over-representation of civil servants in Parliament affects the income distribution between public officials and the rest of society, as well as the allocation of funds between public and private sectors of the economy. Anybody earning his living by market activity and fixing too high a salary for himself runs the risk of becoming uncompetitive for cost reasons and thereby losing customers. The civil servants in Parliament, on the other hand, can fix their own salary without being constrained by such market reactions.

Preference for particular sectors

As discussed in the section above on inflation, the government has a marked tendency to prefer 'producers' (capital-owners and workers) to consumers. The government of course cannot yield to the demands of *all* sectors, because the reason for the resulting inflation and tax increases would be so obvious that the voters as consumers would no longer support the party in power. The question therefore is *which sectors* are benefited by government in the fight over income distribution.

The more that the following three characteristics apply to a particular economic sector, the better are its chances of being supported by a government interested in maintaining its share of votes:

(1) the sector comprises many employees ready to vote for the opposition if they are dissatisfied with the government;

(2) the sector is able considerably to damage the rest of the economy if it finds this to be an effective instrument to use against government;

(3) the sector experiences a slow (below-average) growth of demand for its products. The profit rate of capital-owners and the growth rate of wages of the employees are also below average, so that both feel underprivileged. In addition, employment is threatened further if the enterprises try to increase or at least keep up their profit rate by rationalising. All people employed in the particular sector are more or less informed about this situation, certainly much better informed than those employed in flourishing sectors for which such information is of less importance. Government support for a sector with slowly growing demand is realised much more clearly by the employees concerned and is accordingly rewarded at elections.

Political economy and income distribution

Political economy does not intend to substitute traditional economic theory but rather to enlarge the approach by going beyond the market into the political area. Income may be increased not only by market activity but also by the use of political mechanisms. It is necessary to analyse the way in which political decisions are used to acquire additional income. Over-representation in Parliament and influencing the government dependent on re-election have been used as examples for such a use of the political process.

LITERATURE

The traditional theory of inflation according to the modern state of knowledge is well presented in

> David Laidler and Michael Parkin, 'Inflation: A Survey'. *Economic Journal*, 85 (1975).
> John Flemming, *Inflation*. Oxford University Press, 1976.

Laidler and Parkin in their review explicitly point to the lack of a well-developed political theory of inflation. Some of these aspects are discussed in

> Harry G. Johnson, *Inflation and the Monetarist Controversy*. North Holland, Amsterdam, 1972.

A survey of the traditional theory of income distribution is given in

> Martin Bronfenbrenner, *Income Distribution Theory*. Chicago/New York, 1971.

The relationship between income claims by sectors and government policy is discussed by

> Peter Bernholz, 'Economic Policies in a Democracy'. *Kyklos*, 19 (1966).

Part II

What has Political Economy Achieved?

Modern political economy is not a unified doctrine. It is composed of many variants, which differ with respect to the aim of their analysis and the theoretical approach used.

The second part of this book discusses these variants of political economy. The fourth chapter deals with the *Marxist, system-theoretic* and narrowly *economic* approaches. Two variants are dealt with in separate chapters because of their special importance: the fifth chapter is devoted to the political economy of the Unorthodox; the sixth shows how *neoclassical* methodology can be used to study the basic problems of political decisions, an approach that has been called 'public choice'. The seventh chapter analyses the behaviour of political institutions, parties, government, interest groups, and the civil service.

4. Variants of Political Economy

Over the last few years, political economy has experienced a strong upswing. This renaissance is to a small extent only a return to old theories. Now, however, an attempt is being made to overcome the narrowness of 'pure' economic theory and to accept the inseparability of economics and politics. Different scientific views have led to differences in the formulation of questions, in methodological approach and in conclusions – and thus to variants of political economy.

The modern variants of political economy differ most clearly in two aspects.

(1) *Aim of analysis*. One of the variants restricts itself (almost exclusively) to the critique of current economic theory; namely the Cambridge Capital Theory. Another combines the critique of (neo-)classical theory with the attempt to construct a theory of its own. This applies to the political economy of the New Left (or Radical Economics) and of the Unorthodox. Yet another variant is interested in the development of a new theory combining economics and politics: the social science systems theory, and systems dynamics and public choice. A last variant endeavours to improve government advising; this includes systems analysis and policy science, as well as applied economic policy. Table 4.1 shows the variants mentioned according to the criterion of aims or goals.

(2) *Methodological approach*. The methods used in political economy may be classified according to four criteria. The first variant uses Marxism as a theoretical background. This applies to the New Left and Cambridge Capital Theory (which is, however, also strongly influenced by Ricardo). The second approach uses a non-economic theory, namely systems theory. Here belong the social science systems theory and systems dynamics, as well as systems analysis and policy science. The third and fourth approach

use the foundations of modern economic theory. In the first case traditional neoclassical theory is adopted. This applies to public choice and to applied economic policy. In the second case there is a determined attempt to search for new approaches. This variant is represented by the political economy of the Unorthodox.

Table 4.1 shows the variants mentioned classified according to the methodological approaches given in the top row. By a comprehensive view of the table, i.e. moving at the same time along rows and columns, we can determine the position of each variant with respect to goals *and* methodology used.

TABLE 4.1   *A classification of variants of political economy*

| Aim of analysis | Methodological approach | | | |
	Marxism	Non-economic theory (systems theory)	Neoclassical economic theory	New economic approaches
Critique of existing theory	Cambridge Captial Theory	—	—	—
Critique and new theory	New Left (Radical Economics)	—	—	Unorthodox
Positive theory of economics and politics	—	Social science systems theory and systems dynamics	Public choice	—
Government-advising	—	Systems analysis and policy science	Applied economic policy	—

All the variants mentioned are part of *modern* political economy. Contributions of mostly historical interest are excluded. The same applies to the purely traditional use of the term, such as for example in the name of the *Journal of Political Economy*. Those approaches that are concerned *solely* with the problem of identifying the values inherent in theory are not considered; in that sense all economics is 'political'.

The seven variants of modern political economy classified in Table 4.1 will be discussed in a sequence following the methodological approach:

Marxist approaches
– Cambridge Capital Theory
– New Left

Non-economic approaches
– Social science systems theory and systems dynamics
– Systems analysis and policy science

Traditional economics
– Applied economic policy

The discussion of these variants should serve as a *short* survey and not as a complete representation and final evaluation. The goal is to show the broadness of approaches within modern political economy.

Owing to their special importance, the political economy of the Unorthodox and public choice are treated more extensively in separate chapters. The succeeding chapters present my own approaches, which combine elements of public choice and of the economic theory of the Unorthodox. This combination may be termed 'new political economy'.

MARXIST APPROACHES

Cambridge Capital Theory

The Capital Theory developed in Cambridge seeks to prove the insufficiency of neoclassical economics with its own methods. The basis of the critique lies in the aggregate theories of income distribution according to marginal productivity and of economic growth. For the first time, modern neoclassics is attacked on its own ground. The debate takes place in renowned journals, uses the modern theoretical terminology and demands considerable mathematical knowledge.

The theory questions the following three *basic* neoclassical results.

(1) 'The rate of interest reflects capital's scarcity.' This aspect is of great importance for the use of prices as an allocative (steering) device. The

Cambridge economists deny that a higher capital intensity corresponds to a lower interest–wage rate relation (and conversely).

(2) 'Income distribution is determined by production technology and preferences.' The Cambridge Capital Theory doubts the generality of the macroeconomic marginal productivity theory: income distribution cannot be determined within the economic system, but depends (among others) on power.

(3) 'Aggregate capital and macroeconomic production functions are important and dependable concepts for the analysis of economics, in particular in periods of growth.' The Cambridge Theory proves that, in general, capital cannot be defined independent of the rate of interest (or, alternatively, of the wage rate). Capital cannot be used to determine the rate of interest in all those cases that are of particular interest for the analysis of an actual economy. Neoclassical growth theory, which is based on the macroeconomic production function, becomes open to doubt, as it is true only under very special circumstances, e.g. in a one-good economy with a linear interest–wage relation, or in a dynamically efficient state (i.e. when the conditions of the Golden Rule apply).

The main difference between current neoclassics and the Cambridge Capital Theory lies in the analysis of income distribution. Neoclassics takes goods and factor prices to be simultaneously determined by marginal utility and marginal productivity. The rate of profit (interest), the wage rate and therefore the factor income are derived assuming a capital stock that is given in each instant of time.

Cambridge theoreticians see the process in the reverse order: income distribution is determined outside of the model. The economic system has a degree of freedom. Only if it is closed by a profit mark-up determined by power are goods prices determined. Demand and supply are no longer determined simultaneously: goods prices are fixed by a mark-up on wage costs; demand determines the amount sold. This approach implies that profit has nothing to do with efficiency and hence cannot be justified. Income distribution is the result of extra-economic forces; it is a matter of *political economy*.

It must be added critically that price determination is possible in this way only if there is a *unique* profit rate or mark-up, which can be expected only in perfect competition and *in equilibrium*.

From the point of view of political economy several objections can be raised against Cambridge Capital Theory.

(1) The model assumptions are in many respects extremely neoclassical and therefore are equally distant from reality. Thus it is assumed that there is perfect competition, constant returns to scale and a uniform profit rate.

(2) 'Political economy' restricts itself exclusively to proving that the economic model has a degree of freedom, and that therefore either the profit or the wage rate must be determined outside the model, i.e. 'politically'.

(3) Many adherents of Cambridge Capital Theory quickly and unjustifiably draw the conclusion that if neoclassics may be proved to contain errors, the *only* solution is Marxism. Such a conclusion is, of course, untenable. Some researchers endeavour, however, to develop a non-Marxist theory on the basis of the critique. The most prominent is Kaldor's theory of income distribution and its generalisation by Pasinetti. It reverts to the Keynesian circular flow analysis and derives that the share of profit in national income is in the short run determined by the rates of investment and saving. In the long run the savings propensity of wage-receivers becomes inconsequential. For the other parts of economics there are no well-developed theories as yet; at best there are some preliminary attempts. From the point of view of political economy it is important to note that the non-Marxist approaches do not consider the interdependence between the economy and the polity of a country.

(4) Cambridge Capital Theory claims that the concept of aggregate capital is necessary for a capitalist economy because its value must be known in order to undertake transactions with capital goods. In socialism, it is argued, there is no problem in this respect. This statement is misleading, as it considers only the property aspect in capital goods. Even *without* private property, it is possible to allocate centrally or decentrally. As it is impossible to take *all* decisions centrally, the problem of the co-ordination of the micro- and macro-levels arises. To solve it, in countries without private property it is necessary to know capital values. What matters is not the question of property, but the system of allocation.

The New Left and Radical Economics

The New Left, or as it is now usually called in the United States 'Radical Economics', is the modern variant of Marxist political economy resulting from the student uprisings of the late 1960s. It is difficult to gain a comprehensive view of its contribution as it comprises many factors which partly oppose each other bitterly.

The New Left is based on a critique of traditional neoclassical economics. The following arguments against current theory are dominant:

(1) the specific features of (late-) capitalist economies and the decisive role of monopolies and multinationals are not accounted for;
(2) the central importance of income distribution is neglected in favour of the study of allocative problems; all aspects of power and exploitation remain outside the analysis;
(3) consumers' preferences are taken as given;

(4) quantitative problems in the economy are overstressed, while problems such as alienation are disregarded;
(5) the interdependence between the economy and the polity is not analysed;
(6) social development is wrongly interpreted to be harmonious and in equilibrium;
(7) only marginal changes within a given situation (the capitalist system of production) are considered; the need for and possibility of total change are not studied.

On the basis of the critique of current economics a theory is developed that is intended adequately to reflect capitalist societies. This theory differs in important respects from orthodox Marxism.

(1) The New Left is against authoritarian planning as well as against the open market, whereas the Old Left accords an important role to the former. The New Left is little concerned with the best allocation of scarce means of production among competing ends: resource allocation problems cannot arise because an unselfish 'socialist man' is postulated. The only exception worth mentioning is Mandel's proposal that workers' councils should control production. (It is not specified how the decentralised decisions taken in the enterprises would be co-ordinated).
(2) The New Left advocates the decentralisation of economic and social processes, while the Old Left saw the solution in centralisation.
(3) The New Left does not follow Marxist orthodoxy in its stress upon quantitative increases in production; they rather point to the qualitative aspect.
(4) The leaders of revolution are considered to be not the workers but rather the intellectuals.

Modern Marxist political economy has not only developed general theories of society but has also studied particular areas. The conflict between capital and labour, exploitation by alienation and capital accumulation as the motive power of capitalist development form the core of its tenet. For the New Left, price theory is the analysis of the power struggle between labour and capital for surplus value; business cycle and growth theory describe the crisis of the private ownership system, which arises because of the 'contradiction' between social production and private accumulation and profit; its theory of international trade concerns the imperialistic pressure of monopolies to secure raw material sources and markets for their products, as well as the exploitation of developing countries by capitalist nations.

The New Left's approach to the relationship between economics and politics is of greatest interest. In the theory of 'State Monopolistic Capitalism' (Stamocap) the state is seen as an agent of monopolies; it acts on their behalf as an 'ideal capitalist'. The state is taken to have complete control over the economy which it uses to secure the power of capital in a perishing socioeconomic system.

The less extreme Theory of State Behaviour sees as the main function of the state – in addition to the actions in the interest of capital – the preservation of mass loyalty. The former is sought by furthering accumulation, the latter by a policy of social harmonisation. The instrument available to the state is the civil service with its comprehensive planning, steering and controlling apparatus. The economy and the state are in this view strongly dependent on each other. The capitalist economy requires constant intervention by the state in order to be able to perform its function; the state conversely depends on big industry (and big finance as an arbitrator). Capitalist crises are moreover shifted to the political arena, because the state is made responsible for the stabilisation of economic cycles. As long as capitalism exists, it is not possible to get rid of the fundamental economic conflicts, so that a 'continuous political crisis' exists. The fundamental conflict arises out of the capitalist mode of production, in which production is social but the means of production are private.

The state is in a particularly difficult position because it acts as an agent on behalf of the interest of capital as a whole, while individual capitalists at the same time are pursuing differing interests. Conflicts may also arise between the goal of securing the interests of capital and maintaining legitimacy with the population, especially when the demand for purely material growth is replaced by the desire for an improvement in the (immaterial) quality of life.

The increase in state activity is seen as a cause as well as a consequence of the expansion of monopoly capital. The costs of social investments (in the infrastructure) are increasingly provided by the state, but the surplus is appropriated by the private sector. The power of the state is misused in capitalism for private, particular interests, thereby aggravating economic and political problems.

The charge is made against traditional public finance that as a theory of the ruling (monopolistic) class it does not undertake the study of the true determinants of state activity, but that it is interested only in maintaining existing social and economic conditions.

Many criticisms can be made of the New Left's interpretation of political economy. The school is dogmatically narrow and entirely convinced of the exclusive truth of its doctrine. Capitalist interests are omnipotent – as long as there is no revolution. An empirical test of this view seems to be impossible: if capitalist interests win, their influence is proved; if they do not win, this is evidence of the particularly refined strategy of capital which is capable of *partially* giving up untenable positions in order to maintain their overall influence. The analysis concerns itself almost exclusively with the conditions in a society in which the means of production are privately owned. The New Left does not seriously consider the question of whether the same problems do not also arise in socialist societies. They do not deny that problems observable in reality – such as environmental decay – also can and do occur without private ownership of capital. They do however argue that such similarities are only a 'surface phenomenon'; in a deeper sense the problem is completely different. The approach thus does not permit serious discussion. 'Contradictions' are assumed to reside exclusively in capitalism. A society without private ownership is conversely taken to be one without contradiction. In this respect, the New Left differs but little from utopians and religious dreamers whose ideals are characterised by absence of conflict.

The European New Left has relatively little knowledge of modern economic theory, quite unlike the American Radicals. In Europe, particularly in German-speaking countries, the New Left uses a language of its own which is difficult to understand for the uninitiated. Marx is quoted continuously, and exercises in semantics not infrequently displace the analysis of problems. Serious study is replaced by rhetoric, but it does not suffice to offer *conceptions* which already contain the results.

SYSTEMS THEORETIC APPROACHES TO POLITICAL ECONOMY

Social science systems theory and systems dynamics

Systems theory endeavours to bring together various fields of knowledge including economics and political science, and is therefore considered by some to be political economy. Systems theory provides a unified framework for analysis.

The point of departure is the search for common properties of systems, be they biological, technical or social. A system is a network of relationships the elements of which interact and are connected with elements outside the system. Every change of an element has repercussions on other elements in the system. A system is characterised by continuous changes in the form of adjustment and development processes. The selection of building blocks (elements) is determined by the object or goal of the analysis. A detailed survey of facts is considered necessary. This requires a differentiated terminology.

A system is characterised by certain properties, two of which shall be mentioned here.

(1) Knowledge is an element of the system; i.e., information is of special importance. Consciousness (knowledge about the system) leads to changes in the structural process; i.e., there is a feedback in the form of a use of information. In this way learning can also be taken as an interactive process between the system and its environment.

(2) The behaviour of elements is determined mainly not by individual causal relationships but rather by the total structure of mutual interdependence between the system's elements and their environment. The system as a whole has properties that do not result simply from the 'summation' of isolated components.

Systems theory was originally developed by a biologist for the natural sciences. It is now also used in certain of the social sciences.

(1) In *political science* it forms the basis of the important work of Easton and Deutsch.

(2) In *sociology* and *administrative science* it is particularly used for the analysis of planning in administrations. Bureaucracy is considered to be part of a complicated social environment. The task of administration consists of reducing this complexity. Bureaucracies must be organised in such a way that they are able to fulfil this function according to their own principles. The political process is assumed to adjust to administrative decisions.

(3) In *economics* systems theory plays a modest role, at least in the West. It has received more attention in planned socialist economies.

Systems-theoretic political economy differentiates between inputs and outputs of the political system. Inputs may take the form of demands from the political system but may also consist of inarticulated wishes. Actual political discussion acknowledges only a small number of such demands owing to its limited reception and problem-solving capacity. 'Doormen' – the most important are interest groups, political parties and the civil service – admit only demands favourable to them. In the political sub-system inputs are transformed into outputs. For this purpose certain channels are available. The decisions are the outputs; they may comprise verbal declarations or concrete measures. The consequences of such declarations and actions influence the total system via feedbacks and may lead to new demands *vis-à-vis* the political system through induced preference changes.

The systems-theoretic approach claims to enable a differentiated analysis of political and economic factors and of their relationships to each other. The explicit analysis of the origin and inter-dependence of values draws attention to an aspect disregarded by traditional economics. The weakness of systems theory is that its concepts and postulated relationships are not formulated in such a way that they may be tested empirically. Thus it runs the danger of constructing an elaborate terminological structure of words without meaning, which may impress the uninitiated but contributes little to the understanding of the interaction between economy and polity.

Systems dynamics

Since the publication of the book *Limits to Growth* in the context of the Club of Rome, systems dynamics as a special variant of systems theory has been widely known. It uses large computer models to simulate processes and is, therefore, forced to quantify all concepts. In contrast to the analytical models used in economic theory, such simulation models require much fewer restrictions with respect to the mathematical formulation. As no analytic solution is looked for, in systems-dynamic approaches a great number of dynamic, interdependent and nonlinear relationships between variables may be chosen. The parameter values of the models are not statistically estimated, as in econometrics, but are fixed according to plausi-bility. Owing to the complexity of the social and technological relationships introduced into the analysis, there may be some results that contradict common sense. A disadvantage of systems dynamics is the lack of a theoretical basis, resulting in the tendency to use *ad hoc* assumptions. The complicated approaches not infre-quently reveal prejudice in the disguise of a formalised model.

Systems dynamics is notable for its application of *one* method to all social areas, so that it seems possible to derive a unified political economy. In the existing models by Forrester and Meadows there are, however, no political processes included. In the second stage of the models of the Club of Rome social aspects receive more consideration: 'politics' is introduced in the form of a decision model for statesmen, for which purpose a hierarchical model structure is used. It must be left open whether a (further) opening of global systems dynamics in the direction of political economy (and political ecology) will take place in future.

Systems analysis and policy science

Systems analysis endeavours to reach desired goals by the best choice among a great many possible actions, taking account of all their consequences. It is a practically orientated method of rationalising decision-making. Sometimes it is also referred to as the *theory of political advising*. Systems analysis uses a systematic working plan consisting of three steps:

(1) a narrowing down of the decision problem by an explicit formulation of the problem, careful selection of goals and a broad search for alternatives for political action;
(2) an analysis of the decision problem by data collection, formulation of a (possibly mathematical) model and undertaking of a cost–benefit analysis;
(3) an interpretation and evaluation of the results and, based thereon, a check of assumptions and possibly a revision of goals.

Step (3) leads back to the starting point. The method is planned as an iterative process. Practical applications of systems analysis have shown, however, that an increase in the efficiency of deriving political decisions is not sufficient, because the important step to the actual *taking* of decisions is disregarded. Policy science seeks to overcome this shortcoming of systems analysis.

Policy science is the science of planning political decisions. The main reason for often-disappointing political actions in reality is considered to be not lack of knowledge but rather its insufficient application. Policy science regards itself as a supra-science combining elements of different fields of knowledge in order to bring about better decisions. It adds to systems analysis above all the element of evaluation and improvement of the chance for success of the proposals advanced. For this reason it can rightly be taken to belong to political economy.

Policy science wants to overcome the main shortcomings of political and administrative decision processes. It criticises especially the following three aspects of current decision making.

(1) Problems are defined *too narrowly*. This results in two disadvantages in political decision-making:
– repercussions in other areas are insufficiently accounted for;
– actions appropriate for specific areas are applied to problems for which they are harmful rather than useful.
(2) Social innovation and experiments are neglected.
(3) The recommendations coming from outside (e.g. from experts) are often advanced as fixed proposals ill-suited for the changing requirements of the political power game.

The theory of political advising is built on various paradigms, of which the following differ from the traditional theory of economic policy:

(1) policy science is strongly integrative;
(2) its main goal is overcoming the separation between pure and applied research;
(3) rational as well as extra-rational processes (such as intuition and charisma) are taken account of;
(4) historical developments are given due credit;
(5) dynamic processes and preference changes form an important part of the analysis.

Policy science is a notable attempt to analyse a neglected area of political economy with the help of modern methods. Economics, which is only gradually and reluctantly starting to analyse these aspects, has much to gain from it. This also applies to other variants of political economy that disregard elements such as extra-rational processes and historical developments. Of special importance is the endeavour to develop realisation strategies, practical orientation and thereby the possibility for direct application which is often neglected in other variants of political economy.

At the same time, the theory of political advising can learn from other variants of political economy. It may be argued that it is subject to technocratic illusion: an improvement in the methods for decision-making cannot be expected to guarantee an increase in social rationality.

TRADITIONAL ECONOMICS AS AN APPROACH TO POLITICAL ECONOMY

Applied economic policy

This branch of political economy considers itself concerned with the practical application of economic theory for purposes of government advising, especially in institutions such as the Council of Economic Advisors in the United States and the Sachverständigenrat in the Federal Republic of Germany. Part of the aims of political economy as practical economic policy is also the attempt to bring about incomes policy, 'social contract' or 'concerted action'.

As a rule the economic theory concerned has long been known and accepted in academia but has infrequently or not at all been applied in a political situation. The main task of the members of the Council of Economic Advisors is, even today, trying to teach the President and congressmen the principles of the 'new economics' (i.e. of Keynesian theory). The influence of the various institutionalised interest groups upon economic policy-making is paid special attention, as is the fact that in modern industrial societies public bureaucracy and the various parliamentary commissions try to realise their own interests, which do not necessarily benefit others. This type of political economy is orientated at the immediate problems of everyday economic policy-making. This does not exclude that longer-run aspects are also considered, such as the attempt to rationalise government expenditures with the help of PPBS (Planning–Programming–Budgeting System).

The politico-economic elements can be summarised in two points.

(1) The policy adviser must get involved with individual politicians and their problems in order to be able effectively to communicate 'economic expertise'.
(2) He sees his own political role as spokesman for inarticulate consumer interests against the well-organised groups of producers and trade unions.

In comparison to other variants of political economy, the proponents of practical political advising are rather naïve with respect to the relationship between economics and politics. Conflicts between goals have a tendency to be denied, and unanimity is stressed. It is proclaimed, for example, 'Happily for the economic adviser, politics and economics are often in harmony rather than conflict'; or 'Economists of contrasting political views agree among themselves on many issues'.

The possibilities and the role of the science of economics are evaluated most optimistically, sometimes even euphorically. It is in marked contrast to the scepticism regarding effective government action held by the New Left as well as by other political economists. This scepticism is not unfounded: experience in the United States has shown, for example, that after some time PPBS serves not as an orientation to social goals as intended, but on the contrary as a means by which ministries hope to forward their own interests.

The practical policy variant of political economy thus is in various respects defective. This does not mean that practical government advising and the use of planning instruments should be given up. What is necessary is a stronger theoretical orientation of this practical policy, a renunciation of ill-founded concepts of harmony, and an increased application of *political* economy.

Literature

There are no complete surveys of modern political economy. The useful reader
> E. K. Hunt and Jesse G. Schwartz (eds), *A Critique of Economic Theory*. Penguin, Harmondsworth, 1972

contains mainly Marxist contributions as well as a few articles by adherents of Cambridge Capital Theory and by unorthodox economists.

Cambridge Capital Theory is presented in a readable (but not always precise) way in
> Geoffrey C. Harcourt, *Some Cambridge Controversies in the Theory of Capital*. Cambridge University Press, 1972.

The discussion is put into the general capital-theoretic perspective by
> J. A. Kregel, *Theory of Capital*. Macmillan, London, 1975.

The most important articles (up to 1970) are collected in the reader
> Geoffrey C. Harcourt and N. F. Laing (eds), *Capital and Growth*. Penguin, Harmondsworth, 1971.

A critical survey has recently been given by
> Mark Blaug, *The Cambridge Revolution, Success or Failure*. Institute of Economic Affairs, London, 1975.

The dominant Marxist orientation of Cambridge Capital Theory is represented by
> Amit Bhaduri, 'On the Significance of Recent Controversies of Capital

Theory: A Marxian View'. In G. C. Harcourt and N. F. Laing (eds), op. cit.

The two most important contributions to a non-Marxist development of Cambridge Capital Theory in the area of income distribution are

Nicholas Kaldor, 'Alternative Theories of Distribution'. *Review of Economic Studies*, 23 (1955/56)

Luigi L. Pasinetti, 'Rate of Profit and Income Distribution in Relation to the Rate of Economic Growth'. *Review of Economic Studies*, 29 (1961/62).

A general non-Marxist theory on the basis of the Cambridge critique in current economic theory is attempted by

J. A. Kregel, *The Reconstruction of Political Economy: An Introduction to Post-Keynesian Economics*. London, 1973.

The political economy of the New Left and Radicals in the United States is excellently surveyed by

Martin Bronfenbrenner, 'Radical Economics in America, 1970'. *Journal of Economic Literature*, 8 (1970)

Assar Lindbeck, *The Political Economy of the New Left*. Harper and Row, New York, 1971.

There are no comparable surveys existing of the European New Left.

Two typical contributions of Radical Economics are

Rafer Boddy and James Crotty, 'Class Conflict and Macro-Policy: The Political Business Cycle'. *Review of Radical Political Economics*, 7 (Spring 1975)

Stephen Marglin, 'What Do Bosses Do? The Origins and Functions of Hierarchy in Capitalist Production'. *Review of Radical Political Economics*, 6 (1974).

The German New Left is represented by

Joerg Huffschmid, *Die Politik des Kapitals. Konzentration und Wirtschaftspolitik in der Bundesrepublik*. Edition Suhrkamp, Frankfurt, 1969.

The Neo-Marxist theory of the state is heavily influenced by

James O'Connor, *The Fiscal Crisis of the State*. St Martin's Press, New York, 1973.

The origin of systems theory is

Ludwig V. Bertalanffy, 'General Systems Theory: A New Approach to Unity of Science'. *Human Biology*, 23 (1951).

A social science introduction is given by

Kenneth E. Boulding, *General Systems Theory – The Skeleton of Science*. Reprinted in his book *Beyond Economics*. The University of Michigan Press, Ann Arbor, 1968.

Collections of essays are

F. E. Emery (ed.), *Systems Thinking*. Penguin, Harmondsworth, 1969

H. Bossel, S. Klaczko and N. Mueller (eds), *Systems Theory in the Social Sciences*. Birkhaeuser, Basel/Stuttgart, 1976.

The applications to political science mentioned refer to

David Easton, *A Systems Analysis of Political Life*. Wiley, New York, 1965

Karl W. Deutsch, *The Nerves of Government*. Free Press, New York, 1963.

The sociological variant and application to public administration has mainly been undertaken by

Niklas Luhmann, *Politische Planung. Aufsätze zur Soziologie von Politik und Verwaltung*. Westdeutscher Verlag, Opladen, 1971.

Works applying systems theory to economic problems in planned socialist countries are mentioned in

Janós Kornai, *Anti-Equilibrium*. North Holland, Amsterdam, 1971.

Systems dynamics is due to

Jay W. Forrester, *Industrial Dynamics*. MIT Press, Cambridge, Mass., 1961.

Better known is the first study of the Club of Rome

Dennis H. Meadows *et al.*, *The Limits to Growth*. Universe Books, New York, 1972.

The second report to the Club of Rome has been prepared by

Mihajlo Mesarovíc and Eduard C. Pestel, *Menschheit am Wendepunkt*. Deutsche Verlags-Anstalt, Stuttgart, 1974.

Systems analysis is covered in the reader

S. L. Optner (ed.), *Systems Analysis*. Penguin, Harmondsworth, 1973.

Policy science has been strongly shaped by

Yehezkel Dror, *Design for Policy Sciences*. American Elsevier, New York, 1971.

Typical proponents of political economy as applied economic policy are

Walter W. Heller, *New Dimensions of Political Economy*. Norton, New York, 1967

Arthur M. Okun, *The Political Economy of Prosperity*. Norton, New York, 1970.

The sentences quoted in the text are by Heller (p. 17) and Okun (p. 1).

5. The Unorthodox

Unorthodox economists such as Galbraith and Myrdal are among a small number of scientists well-known both to laymen and to researchers in other subjects. The Galbraithian view of the dominance of large enterprises and the interconnection between the military–industrial complex and the state is probably shared by the great majority of social scientists – except for economists, who often do not take it seriously or even express contempt for the idea. Modern economic theory built upon neoclassicism does not attribute special importance to (large) enterprises compared with consumers; rather, the economic process is assumed to be guided by the wishes of consumers; the enterprises have to adjust to consumer preferences. As I have stressed above, current economic theory disregards the interaction between the economy and the polity.

So far, the Unorthodox have not been understood as a movement of their own within the science of economics. The reason may lie in the fact that they often differ considerably from one another with respect to conceptions and conclusions. The approaches are usually shaped by the personality of the respective researchers in an unmistakable way. Schools are formed only in exceptional cases.

COMMON TRAITS

The most prominent characteristic of unorthodox political economy is the combination of a criticism of current theory and its substitution by new and original ideas. The goal is to overcome the narrowness of neoclassicism by innovative thoughts. From the point of view of modern political economy this enterprise deserves special

attention. It is possible to find common traits in the criticisms of
established economics and the new approaches.

Criticisms of current economic theory

The Unorthodox above all criticise the irrelevance of many questions treated by neoclassical economists. Instead of a search for
solutions to important problems in society, neoclassicists dwell on
discussions within the science resulting in small refinements of
existing abstract models. It is in this 'high' and 'pure' theory that
scientific merits may be gained, and so the occupation with practical
questions of economic policy is by comparison little esteemed.

The scientific discussion within this abstract world of models does
not force neoclassical economists to reconsider basic assumptions
such as perfect competition between very small firms, the steering
of production by the all-powerful consumers, unchanged preferences of ecomomic men and constant economies of scale. The
Unorthodox consider such assumptions to be completely unrealistic, and to give a wrong perspective of modern industrial society.
They also object to the importance given to allocation, considering the economy not to be exclusively or even mainly concerned
with the best use of scarce resources among competing ends. The
separation between allocation and income distribution often to be
found in neoclassical thinking is also rejected.

New approaches

The following six assumptions are common to unorthodox economists.

(1) The economy is part of a *socio-cultural system*. It is formed by it and at
the same time it influences culture and society. The economy can, therefore, be understood only in a *trans-disciplinary* way. In this sense, the
Unorthodox are political economists. The relationship between
economy and polity is taken into account by considering the interaction
of the two sectors. An intensive study of political processes is however
rarely undertaken.
(2) Institutions play a major role in economic life. One of the most
important of such institutions are large enterprises or trusts: they dominate economic activity while consumers have little influence.
(3) Power and conflict are central elements in economy and society. For
this reason income distribution is considered very important.

(4) Economic development is *evolutionary*; i.e., it takes place over time and may not be turned backwards. It is characterised by cumulative processes. Disequilibria are able to bring out creative forces and are, therefore, welcome. The major determinants of economic growth are technology and knowledge, as well as preference changes.

(5) Problems of developing countries and disadvantaged regions within rich countries are the subject of intensive analysis and political engagement.

(6) *Relevance* is taken to be of greater importance than rigour from the point of view of methodology. An attempt is made to grasp the large problems even if they are beyond formal analysis.

THE CONTRIBUTION OF PARTICULAR RESEARCHERS

The political economy of the Unorthodox can best be discussed by considering the contributions of individual researchers. Only the Institutionalists formed a kind of school of their own. Between 1890 and 1920 they occupied a prominent position in America. Their best-known representatives were John R. Commens, Wesley C. Mitchell and Thorstein B. Veblen. Their contributions, however, differed markedly from each other. The most original among them is Veblen whose work is therefore sketched below.

John K. Galbraith, Albert O. Hirschman and Kenneth E. Boulding in the United States are worthy successors of these early unorthodox economists. In Europe, Gunnar Myrdal keeps up the flag of institutionalism. United in their fight against the theory of general (economic) equilibrium are the Frenchman François Perroux, the Hungarian János Kornai and the Englishman Nicholas Kaldor; each of whom tries to develop economics in a different direction. In German-speaking countries it is difficult to name economists who are unorthodox in the same way as the scientists just mentioned – probably because neoclassicism, which serves as an antithesis, could never claim the same dominance as in (especially) Anglo-Saxon countries. As an example of another type of unorthodoxy, the political economy of which is rooted in history, the work of Edgar Salin (a German–Swiss economist) is discussed.

The unorthodox economists discussed below are an incomplete sample; no full treatment is intended. Rather, an impression shall be given of the contribution of some of the best-known representatives of unorthodox political economy. Schumpeter's work is deliberately not treated here; his idea of democracy in the form of party competition makes him a precursor of the economic theory of politics (covered in the next two chapters); his other contributions are, moreover, ably covered in the history of doctrines. His concepts of dynamic entrepreneurs and of the process of creative destruction surely put him among unorthodox political economists. The same applies to John Maynard Keynes, who in theory and practical politics always considered the economy to be part of society. His normative conception of government, however, is élitist: experts are supposed to guide economic policy optimally in the interests of the society as a whole. In this respect, Keynes remains dominated by the idea of a 'benevolent dictator'.

Thorstein Veblen

This unconventional and even eccentric economist endeavoured to free himself from the chains of rational thinking imposed by the classical economists. In place of mechanistic behavioural assumptions, he tried to capture the hidden motivations of human action by using anthropological perspectives. For example, the behaviour of the 'leisure class' is emulated by the members of lower strata in society; the accumulation of money and its ostentatious use are regarded as indications of social position; work, on the other hand, is considered to be without dignity or even degrading. Using man's tendency for imitation, Veblen tries to explain why in North America the oppressed do not overthrow the capitalist class according to Marxian predictions. The position of the 'leisure class' cannot be upheld owing to its failure to participate in the production process. The engineers take over.

With this view Veblen advances some thoughts that later play a major role in the work of Galbraith and other unorthodox economists. The main emphasis in his theory lies in the explanation of the changes in consumer preferences and the passing of the market form from small to large enterprises with dominating managers. He does not, however, make any important contribution to the analysis of the relationship between government and economy.

John Kenneth Galbraith

Owing to his richness of ideas, his occupation with important problems and his strong influence among non-professional economists, Galbraith takes a most prominent place among economists. His theories, which differ markedly from traditional neoclassics and which are partly radical, make him an outsider – a position he enjoys greatly. As a liberal he calls not for a revolution but rather for reforms to improve the present social order.

Galbraith's analytical approach is opposite to that of neoclassical economics: while the latter is concerned with the market, he argues that the price system no longer serves well as a mechanism of co-ordination and that it must be substituted by planning. In the place of atomistic firms in perfect competition, the large enterprise is taken to be representative for modern times. Consumer sovereignty is taken over by producer sovereignty, and instead of the size of gross national product it is its composition that is taken to be important. Galbraith thus endeavours to make assumptions that are valid for the twentieth century.

Central to his thinking are the big firms or trusts whose behaviour is determined by top personnel – in Galbraith's word, the 'techno-structure'. The prime goal of this management is to remain in its position of power; the shareholders play only an unimportant role. Large corporations use the most modern technology, requiring continually increasing outlays of capital and a lengthening of the production process. To master the resulting problems the techno-structure needs to plan not only the production process but also sales. In modern capitalism, planning is as necessary as in socialist economies without private ownership of the means of production. The two systems dominated by oligarchies become more and more similar.

The trusts guarantee the sale of their product by manipulating consumers through advertising. The consumers' needs are con-tinually enhanced by the production process, which should actually satisfy them. Consumers' wishes become completely subservient to producers' interests. Strong advertising for private goods leads to a neglect of public goods, which must be supplied by the community as a whole: private squander goes with public poverty.

The large corporations forming the 'planning system' dominate economy and society. Small- and medium-sized firms operating in the 'market system' have no power and must passively adjust.

The political system is also subservient to big enterprises. The state is an executive organ of the large firms. Its task is to guard against over-production by securing demand. Of special importance is the 'military–industrial complex', which combines private and state interests.

Galbraith's ideas have changed over time. According to his first works, the power of big corporations is diminished by the appearance of 'countervailing power', particularly in the form of trade unions. In his newer writings the workers are considered to be well-paid adherents of the planning system. Also, the 'scientific estate' composed of the educational interests no longer plays a major role as an opponent of the techno-structure.

Galbraith's views can be criticised in a great many respects. Even monopolistic corporations are not able completely to evade market forces. Their planning does not serve as a substitute for the market but rather as a means to best use it. The important difference between planning within the big firms and planning as a substitute of the price system is overlooked. Galbraith is incapable of showing an alternative to the co-ordination system of the market (which he declares dead). The view of complete power of the planning system – especially with regard to advertising – is untenable.

Galbraith's style of reasoning, which pretends to grasp society in a total and simultaneous way and which is intuitive and impressionistic, does not admit falsification of the hypotheses advanced and is thus in conflict with the requirements of scientific analysis as advanced by Popper. However, even strong critics of Galbraith's views cannot help admiring his originality, his sense for relevant problems, his eloquence and his capacity for discourse with the public.

Albert O. Hirschman

Economic resources such as capital and labour are not given, but must rather be wakened by *creative forces* – this is Hirschman's central conception. The real scarcity is not with respect to resources as such, but only with respect to their uses. The key to economic development lies in the mobilisation of latent social forces.

The state can bring about the preconditions for inducing these creative reactions by deliberately producing infrastructural disequilibria, which will foster the process of development. An oversupply of infrastructure has an ignition function; private entrepreneurs are induced to undertake investments. When there is a

shortage of infrastructure stimuli for overcoming the resulting problems arise, both in the private and public sector.

As an analogy to Adam Smith's 'invisible hand' of the price
system, Hirschman develops the notion of a 'hiding hand'. Man
systematically underestimates his creativity when confronted with
new problems. He realises his power for innovation only when the
solution has already been found. To solve future problems, inherent
difficulties should be presented by the planners as more simple than
they are in reality. This will result in programmes being undertaken
that later turn out to be more difficult than expected. These difficulties, however, exactly awaken those unknown creative forces
required to successfully accomplish the task.

Among the various strategies for wakening latent forces, *political*
reactions are put on equal footing with *market* reactions. There are
mechanisms outside the price system that are also capable of solving
economic problems. In Chapter 2 the social decision systems of *exit*
– the substitution on a market – and of *voice* – the political protest –
have been mentioned. In this respect Hirschman makes an interesting contribution to political economy: the political notion of
opposition is fruitfully applied to the economic sphere. The reverse
procedure to that in public choice is used where economic tools and
thinking are applied to the political sphere. Hirschman's importance as a political economist lies in his capacity intimately to
combine the analysis of economic and political processes.

Kenneth E. Boulding

This scientist fascinates by a fullness of original and unconventional
thoughts about various problems of our time. The economic style of
thinking always remains perceptible. Owing to his diversity he is
difficult to grasp; his strength lies less in a deep analysis of particular
questions than in suggesting new perspectives.

In his analysis of power and conflict he endeavours to show that
economics may usefully be applied to areas that are usually dealt
with only by sociologists or sociologically orientated political
scientists. But he also considers economic theory to be deficient in
important aspects. The assumption of complete selfishness of traditional welfare economics constitutes a misrepresentation of man.
Even exchange requires a minimum of mutual trust. Many social
relationships are strongly characterised by benevolence. Excep-

tionally good men can exert great influence, but even with ordinary people, and even in politics, mutual goodwill is important. Part of the transfers or grants not based on exchange may be explained by this human characteristic. On the other hand, malevolence should not be left out of account. Based on these ideas, Boulding develops a trinitary social organisation system of love, exchange and threat (see Chapter 2).

Economic development is seen as an *evolutionary* process, the essential elements of which are learning and the increase of knowledge. Little is known about learning on the social level. It is in any case quite different from individual learning; in particular, there is a much greater danger of pathological outcomes. In economic development information and communication are important. Knowledge is interpreted as a structured *loss* of information, i.e. a concentration on the essential aspects. Preference change is a normal accompanying phenomenon of growth and may not, therefore, be excluded as it is in traditional welfare theory.

Like Hirschman, Boulding considers *dissatisfaction* with reigning conditions to be the prerequisite for progress. Individual reactions consist of adjustments within the existing system; political reactions consist of a change of the system itself. Political processes differ markedly depending on whether they occur in a growing, a stagnant or even a shrinking economy. Economy and polity may not be looked at in separation; allocation (the traditional economic sphere) is intimately connected with distribution (the traditional political sphere). Political organisations must use the threat system to survive; a large part of transfers, namely taxes, rely on this principle.

Gunnar Myrdal

This Swedish Nobel prize winner deplores the irrelevance and sterility of present neoclassical economics. Much of what is praised as great theory is in retrospect a temporary aberration. Myrdal proposes a view based on *institutionalism, trans-disciplinarity* and *evolution*. The values must openly be shown and should not be arbitrary; pragmatic standards may be relevance and practicability.

The stable equilibrium is an ill-suited instrument for the analysis of complex and dynamic systems. This requires a theory of *circular* and *cumulative causation*. Instability and cycles are intimately connected with historical development, both in industrial nations (where the large corporations are the main cause) and in developing nations. The price system can fulfil only part of the required social functions; it does not take into account all information and therefore is no reliable indicator of individual and social welfare. Social benefit and cost cannot be analysed as small deviations from the price system, as is done in traditional theory – rather, they influence the whole social network.

Myrdal is only marginally concerned with particular political institutions and processes. In his view political economy consists of the attempt to uncover normative elements in economics and to consider the economy as part of a socio-cultural system (to which polity and government belong).

Beyond general equilibrium: François Perroux, Janós Kornai and Nicholas Kaldor

These three scientists are in agreement in their vehement criticism of the model of general equilibrium but they take different points of departure to develop their own theories.

Perroux

François Perroux accuses the theory of general equilibrium of disregarding non-market relationships such as power and the role of groups. The result is not a simplification but a negation of reality. Most economic actors are members of groups characterised by power relations and political strife. This applies particularly to large corporations and financial consortia. If this use of power is taken into account, private and general interests conform only in extreme cases. With respect to income distribution, economic and political power play an important role. The state is required to contain the continuous struggle for power by the groups. It posits the rules and protects those institutions serving the interests of the upper class. Moreover, it must prevent conflicts that are so severe that they threaten to endanger public order.

Kornai

Janós Kornai's critique of the theory of general equilibrium is especially noteworthy as he himself is an insider of this particular research area. His attack is not directed against its logic but is concerned with its relevance: as a representation of the working of an economy it is boring, over-schematic, and even miserable. It does not contribute to an understanding of the economic phenomena found in reality. Its weaknesses are basic; they concern the kind of questions asked, the assumptions and the concepts used. The price system analysed by such models forms only *one* component of a complex control and information system.

To Kornai, disequilibrium is not solely a methodological concept but rather a relevant state of the economy. *Pressure* and *suction* lead to tension, which in turn creates an environment suitable for desirable developments. Pressure should not be identified with excess supply, and suction not with excess demand, because the latter terms refer only to the price system. In disequilibrium information is of special importance. Kornai is not, however, able to derive a closed theory on these foundations; he does not analyse more closely the relationship between economy and polity.

Kaldor

Nicholas Kaldor also accuses the general equilibrium theory of painting a completely false picture of the economy. The development of this branch of theory constitutes a downfall in economics compared with the nineteenth century. The crucial mistake was committed when value theory, with its exclusive interest in the allocative function of the market, started to dominate, and when the creative function of the market as an instrument for the transmission of impulses was neglected.

According to Kaldor, modern economies are characterised by *increasing returns to scale.* The view of the economic process being the allocation of scarce resources breaks down (except in the very short run); external constraints are overcome by endogenous changes. The larger is the growth in production, the smaller are average costs and the more rapidly can capital accumulation proceed. The combination of increasing returns to scale and Keynesian income-creation results in a cumulative process in which macro-economic demand and supply feed on each other. The differentiation between full employment (i.e. a constraint effected by the supply of resources) and unemployment (i.e. a constraint effected by insufficient demand) that is made in traditional economic theory is of no use.

Kaldor's theory certainly is unorthodox, but the step towards a political economy in the sense of an integration of economy and polity is not undertaken.

Edgar Salin

With a background in the European humanistic tradition, Salin endeavours to make the historical dimension and the sociological view fruitful for the problems of our time. In his approach historical and sociological concepts, theory and facts are not introduced in isolation but are closely interwoven. The problems dealt with cover a wide spectrum from a concentration of enterprises to economic and political integration and to the role of new technologies and automation.

Salin's way of thinking is illustrated by his analysis of *concentration*. The merger of firms to larger units is a concomitant phenomenon and a result of technical progress. It is therefore inevitable; economic policy can only try to achieve an optimal degree of concentration. With this thesis Salin is in strong opposition to neo-liberal economics such as those theoretically advanced in Germany by Eucken and Röpke, and in practice applied by the founding father of the 'free market economy', Erhard. For the late phases of capitalism large enterprises are typical; they constitute the strongest force for economic progress. The inevitability as well as the objectivation of the function of large corporations undermine the meaning of property. The rights over private property are reduced and at the same time losses are socialised. The leaders in private and public enterprises are trustees; they become independent of shareholders. The *managers* gain economic and political power. Hand in hand, the employees and workers of large corporations take the status of public officials.

Salin's political economy is concerned with the origins and consequences of economic and political forces and only marginally with political institutions. As in Myrdal's analysis, the political element is regarded as consisting of the way in which society is looked at. In Salin's view the 'pure' theory of the classics (especially of Ricardo) which is separated from institutions contains strong political elements, because it proceeds by strong abstractions and by isolating parts instead of looking at 'the whole'.

EVALUATION

This survey of the various unorthodox economists has shown the diversity and even the marked wilfulness of their approaches. In various respects there is also a consensus: economic development is an evolutionary process; disequilibria are able to awake creative forces, big corporations and managers have strong power and are, to a large extent, able to determine the economic process; technology and consumer preferences are the result of the interdependence of economy and society.

Some of the Unorthodox – especially Hirschman, and to a lesser extent also Boulding, Perroux and Galbraith – develop explicit theories of the relationship between economic and political forces and institutions, in particular between big companies, interest groups and the state. What matters more is the impetus they give for a political economy endeavouring to overcome the narrowness of present neoclassical theory with respect to both *content* and *methodology*. The orientation towards reality, trans-disciplinarity and the sense for dynamics that characterises the Unorthodox can greatly benefit political economy.

LITERATURE

Thorstein Veblen's description of the behaviour of the upper class is to be found in
  Theory of Leisure Class. Random House, New York, 1961 (1st edn 1899).
The taking over of power by engineers is discussed in
  The Theory of Business Enterprise. The American Library, New York, 1904.
John Kenneth Galbraith develops his idea of countervailing power in
  American Capitalism. Harvard University Press, Cambridge, Mass., 1952.
A more stringent critique of society and the idea of reversed sequence (producer sovereignty in the place of consumer sovereignty) and of public poverty is in his famous book
  The Affluent Society. Houghton Mifflin, Boston, 1958.
The central importance of techno-structure and of the planning system is argued in
  The New Industrial State. Houghton Mifflin, Boston, 1967.

A synthesis of the three works is given in
Economics and the Public Purpose. Houghton Mifflin, Boston, 1973.
An excellent critique of Galbraith's work is
Gérard Gäfgen, 'On the Methodology and Political Economy of Galbraithian Economics'. *Kyklos*, 27 (1974).
Albert O. Hirschman's central idea of the awakening of creative forces by producing disequilibria is to be found in
The Strategy of Economic Development. Yale University Press, New Haven, 1958.
The possibility of problem solution via the 'hiding hand' is argued in the article
'The Principle of the Hiding Hand'. *Public Interest*, 6 (1967).
A comparison of economic and political forces is given in
Exit, Voice and Loyalty. Harvard University Press, Cambridge, Mass., 1970.
Kenneth E. Boulding's discussion of power and conflict is in
Conflict and Defense: A General Theory. Harper and Row, New York, 1962.
Important articles are collected in
Beyond Economics. Essays on Society, Religion and Ethics. University of Michigan Press, Ann Arbor, 1968
Economics as a Science. McGraw Hill, New York, 1970.
Gunnar Myrdal's important articles are collected in
Against the Stream. Critical Essays on Economics. Vintage Books, New York, 1975.
A good presentation of this kind of unorthodox political economy is given by
K. William Kapp, 'In Defense of Institutionalism'. *Swedish Journal of Economics*, 70 (1968).
François Perroux's critique of general equilibrium theory and an attempt to take account of power relations are to be found in
L'Economie du XXe Siècle. Presses Universitaires de France, Paris, 1969.
Another unorthodox French contribution is by
Jacques Attali and Marc Guillaume. *L'Anti-Economique*. Presses Universitaires de France, Paris, 1974.
Janós Kornai's main work is
Anti-Equilibrium. North Holland, Amsterdam, 1971.
Nicholas Kaldor has developed his theories particularly in the following articles:
'The Irrelevance of Equilibrium Economics'. *Economic Journal*, 82 (1972)
'What is Wrong with Economic Theory?' *Quarterly Journal of Economics*, 89 (1975).
Edgar Salin has collected his papers in
Lynkeus – Gestalten und Probleme aus Wirtschaft und Gesellschaft. Mohr (Siebeck), Tübingen, 1963.

6. Public Choice

THE THEORETICAL APPROACH

Public choice is a new area of research. It does not yet have a fixed name but is known under various denominations. Sometimes, it is just called 'political economy'; in the United States it is usually called 'public choice'; in Europe the name 'economic theory of politics' is more generally accepted. For the part dealing with the abstract and axiomatic problem of preference aggregation the names 'social choice' or 'collective choice' are used. Having the same content as 'public choice' but directed more towards political science are the names 'mathematical political science' or 'positive political theory'.

Public choice is the *application of the methods of modern economics to the study of political processes.* Public choice seeks to combine economics and politics. One may even say that, owing to the uniformity of methods used, the distinction between the traditional subjects of economics and political science becomes meaningless.

The propounders of public choice have famous economists as predecessors: Wicksell, who studied decision-making rules, and Schumpeter, who advanced the hypothesis of vote-maximising governments. Its development as a research area in its own right, however, began in the 1960s. It is marked by the publication of a few books, namely:

– Arrow's book on the possibilities of the aggregation of individual preferences to a social welfare function;
– Black's research on the properties of the simple majority voting rules;
– Downs's theory of party competition;
– Buchanan and Tullock's study on the choice of rules on the constitutional level;

and finally
– Olson's theory of groups.
These books have strongly influenced the subsequent development.
Public choice has been enriched by various fields within economics.

(1) From *microeconomic theory* the assumptions about the individual's calculus of decision are derived. It is assumed that the individual acts in a rational and generally also selfish way both in the economic and political areas. The behavioural motivation is the same whether the individual acts as producer or consumer, as politician or taxpayer.
(2) From *public finance*, particularly in its continental tradition, stems the occupation with the theory of public goods and externalities which plays a prominent role within public choice.
(3) Strongly influenced by *welfare economics* is the discussion over the existence of a social welfare function, one of the basic problems of political theory. The criterion of Pareto-optimality basic to welfare economics finds its analogy in the requirement of unanimity in democratic decisions.
(4) The methodology of public choice is strongly influenced by *game theory*, which was initially applied to economic problems but which proves to be more useful for the analysis of political questions.
(5) The advances made in empirically testing the theoretical hypotheses developed in public choice – which may be called 'politometrics' – are mainly due to the foundations laid in *econometrics*. In principle, there are the same statistical problems as in economic models, such as the problems of specifying equations, multicollinearity and bias owing to simultaneity of relationships.

In addition to public choice, there are other fields in economics applying the same tools to new areas:

(1) *public economics*, which differs from traditional public finance in its emphasis on the expenditure side of the budget and the functioning of the public sector;
(2) *the theory of property rights*, which extends exchange theory by introducing extra-economic elements into individual utility functions and by taking account of transactions costs: it studies particularly the incentive effects of different property allocations;
(3) *the theory of grants*, which studies one-sided transfers.

These areas all belong to *non-market economics*, which deals with those areas in which there is scarcity, but where the use of the means available is not steered by the price system. With respect to content, it covers such areas as education, health, leisure, crime and peace. One may thus speak of an 'economic approach to social questions'.

This chapter shows how the basic problems of political action are seen from the point of view of public choice. The basic problems are so general that they are independent of particular institutions. A simple introduction is given, and it is demonstrated that particular aspects of this theory also have practical applications.

PREFERENCE AGGREGATION AND THE PARADOX OF VOTING

Politics can be looked at as a procedure to come to social, i.e. *collective*, decisions on the basis of *individual* preferences. It is of central importance to take into account the wishes of the individual members of society because otherwise there would exist a dictatorship of a person or a group, or decisions would be arbitrary. Preference aggregation is considered by many social scientists to be the most important part of public choice because it is the most basic: all social decision-making mechanisms are procedures to aggregate non-homogeneous preferences (unless one holds an organic conception of the state).

In democracies, voting is the most significant procedure for deriving social decisions from the preferences of the individuals. The formal theory of voting analyses the relationship between voting rules and the properties required for a social decision. The requirements upon the welfare function or upon social decisions (also called 'criteria' or 'conditions') may be of a wide variety but always start from a value judgement. A collective decision is 'sensible' only if it meets certain logical conditions.

The paradox of voting

An important question is whether it is *possible* to construct an aggregate welfare function. Some notable scientists such as Borda (in 1781), Condorcet (in 1785), Laplace and Dodgson (professor of mathematics in Oxford, and better known as Lewis Carroll, author of *Alice in Wonderland*) have early come to the conclusion that simple majority voting can lead to such contradictions that reasonable welfare functions cannot be constructed.

The problem can be illustrated with a fable by Aesop. A miller and his son are on the way to town with their donkey. A group of children whom they meet laugh at them because they are walking instead of riding. Thereupon the miller lets his son ride the donkey.

When some old men see this they lament that old age is not accorded due respect and tell the son to change places with his father. As soon as they have done this they meet some women, who insult the father because he lets his poor little son walk while he rides. Thereupon the father lets his son ride together with him. Shortly before they reach their goal they meet some townspeople who reproach them because the donkey has to carry such a heavy weight: the two of them would be better able to carry the donkey than the other way around. Thereupon they both dismount and carry the donkey, to the laughter of the whole town.

Disregarding the last possibility, which obviously is donkeyish, there are four choice options:
A (both walk), B (the son rides, the father walks), C (the father rides, the son walks), D (father and son both ride).

The complete preference order of the groups that father and son meet, probably looks like the following:

children	B>D>A>C
old men	C>D>A>B
women	D>B>C>A
townspeople	A>B>C>D.

B>D, for example, means that alternative B is (ordinally) preferred to alternative D. The miller cannot rely on an unequivocal opinion, i.e. cannot find a consistent majority for any of the actions because (with equal group size and simple majority rule) it is true that

A=B, B>C, C=D, D>A (D=B, C=A).

The equality sign indicates that the vote is undecided. The persons considering themselves as the judges cannot decide as a collectivity between A and B (two of the four groups prefer A to B and two, B to A); B is preferred to C by three of the four groups; C and D are valued equally; and D is again preferred to the first alternative A (three of the four groups prefer D to A)! This result is paradoxical.

The paradox of voting is usually illustrated by an example of three voters (I, II, III) and three alternatives (A, B, C). The individual preferences are assumed to be

Voters	Preferences		
	highest	*medium*	*lowest*
I	A	B	C
II	C	A	B
III	B	C	A

Using simple majority voting, A is preferred to B twice (by voters I and II) and B is preferred to A once (voter III); also, B is preferred to C twice (by voters I and III) and C is preferred to B once (voter II). Upon this result, logical consistency (so-called transitivity) would demand that the voters prefer alternative A to alternative C. A direct vote between A and C results in a paradoxical outcome however because C is preferred to A by voters II and III, while only voter I prefers A to C.

The relevance of the voting paradox lies in the impossibility of finding an unequivocal winner. Alternative A, which seems to be the winner in the beginning, is beaten by C, and that alternative again by B, and that again by A. For this reason one also speaks of *cyclical majorities*. In reality it is often unknown whether there exists a cycle because voting is usually broken off when a winner (in our example A) is found. The outcome can therefore be irrational and arbitrary because it may be that the *order* in which the alternatives are presented is decisive, rather than individual preferences and the democratic procedure. There are obvious possibilities for manipulation.

The Impossibility Theorem

Inconsistent social decisions do not appear only when a simple majority rule is used. The *general* proof of the possibility of paradoxical social decision goes back to Arrow's path-breaking work, which forms the basis of all modern work on the problem of preference aggregation. Arrow sets four conditions that the social welfare function derived from individual preferences must meet:

(1) all logically possible individual preference orderings are admitted (Unrestricted Domain);
(2) if each individual prefers an alternative x to an alternative y, so should society (Pareto Criterion);
(3) the social decision between two alternatives should depend on individual preferences regarding these two (and not other) alternatives (Independence of Irrelevant Alternatives);
(4) no individual should exclusively determine the social decision (Non-dictatorship).

Applying mathematical logic, Arrow proves that these intuitively acceptable conditions are incompatible with each other; in general, there exists no social welfare function. This Impossibility Theorem holds for *all* known and (still) unknown decision methods based on binary comparisons, and not only for majority voting.

The Impossibility Theorem is often wrongly interpreted as implying that logical inconsistencies must *always* appear. This conclusion is wrong; the theorem only proves that such unstable results cannot be excluded with certainty.

The *probability* of having inconsistent social decisions has been calculated with the help of Monte Carlo simulations and also with analytical formulations for the special case of majority voting. It is assumed that each logically possible preference ordering is equally likely. This assumption is rather arbitrary; a society is, on the contrary, characterised by a special distribution of preferences.

Table 6.1 shows the probability with which the voting paradox arises under the conditions mentioned.

TABLE 6.1 *Probability of no majority winner assuming equidistribution of preferences*

No. of alternatives	No. of individuals						
	3	5	7	13	25	59	∞
	%	%	%	%	%	%	%
3	5.56	6.94	7.5	8.11	8.43	8.63	8.77
4	11.11	14	15				17.55
6	20	25	27				31.52
∞							72.97

In the 'textbook' case of three alternatives and three voters, the probability of simple majority voting leading to inconsistent results is less than 6 per cent. The probability rises with both the number of alternatives and the number of voters. If a very large number (more precisely an infinite number) of voters must reach a majority decision among six alternatives, the probability is 31.5 per cent that they will not be able to find a stable solution. With also a very large number of alternatives (more precisely an infinite number of alternatives) among which to choose, this probability rises to almost 73 per cent.

Arrow's Impossibility Theorem has received a great deal of attention, as it shows that democratic decisions can lead to logically contradictory social decisions. His result has been criticised and extended in various directions by subsequent scientific discussion. The four main directions are as follows.

(1) The search for a *normative social* welfare function is considered to be fundamentally mistaken. It is therefore of no importance whether such a function can be formulated in a consistent way. A social welfare function is of interest only to a dictator or an élite; for a democratic society the process and institutions that determine when and how individuals act collectively must be analysed. This view corresponds to the idea of *constitutional contract* (discussed in Chapter 2).

(2) The Impossibility Theorem is accepted but inconsistencies of democratic decisions are not considered a defect. As the theorem also applies to majority voting, it makes a consistent exploitation of the minority by the majority impossible.

(3) In place of a social welfare function implying transitivity of social decisions, a social decision function is taken as the goal. This function implies acyclicity only (i.e. if x_1 is better than x_2, x_2 better than x_3, . . . x_{n-1} better than x_n, then x_1 should not be worse than x_n). It can be shown that the four Arrow conditions are in that case logically compatible with each other. However, as soon as another weak criterion is introduced, no such social decision-making function exists.

(4) The Arrow conditions that preference aggregation should meet are changed when the aim becomes one of enabling the derivation of a non-contradictory social decision-making function. For that purpose all four conditions are at our disposition but the Pareto Criterion and Non-dictatorship are so obvious that it would be unreasonable to change them. The discussion has, therefore, been concerned mainly with the criteria of Unrestricted Domain and Independence of Irrelevant Alternatives.

The next section deals with the various possibilities and consequences of giving up the condition of Unrestricted Domain of individual preferences. This is followed by a consideration of vote-trading, which is possible when differences in preference intensity exist. Such differences may be taken into account when the condition of Independence of Irrelevant Alternatives is given up.

Restriction on individual preference orderings

If all individuals have the same preferences, there exists no aggregation problem. The question is, what deviation from unanimity of individual preferences is tolerable so that the impossibility result does not apply?

Single-peakedness is the best-known restriction on individual preference orderings. In a graphical presentation of alternatives available, there is at least one arrangement in which each preference order has only *one* 'peak'. The example given above with three voters and three alternatives is illustrated in Figure 6.1.

The preference line of voter II has two peaks (with alternatives A and C); therefore, the requirement of single-peakedness is not met. In the other five possible arrangements of the three alternatives, there is always one voter whose preference line has two peaks.

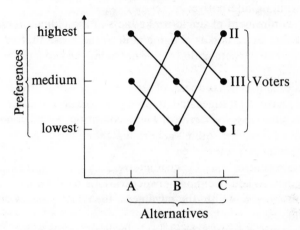

FIG. 6.1. *Absence of single-peakedness*

The following preference orderings, in which voter II's preference is substituted by IIa, yields a single-peaked arrangement (Figure 6.2):

$$
\begin{array}{ll}
\text{I} & A>B>C \\
\text{IIa} & B>A>C \\
\text{III} & B>C>A
\end{array}
$$

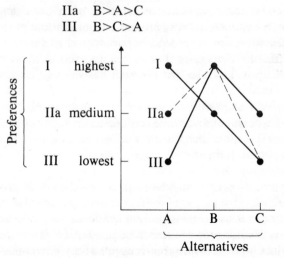

FIG. 6.2. *Single-peaked preference ordering*

A majority vote yields a victory of B over A and of A over C, from which it can reasonably be deduced that alternative B is preferred to alternative C. A direct vote between B and C shows, indeed, that B is the winning alternative.

The requirement of single-peakedness of individual preferences implies that there is partial agreement in the sense that everyone agrees on one particular alternative not being the worst (in our case, alternative B).

Besides single-peakedness, other restrictions on individual preferences have been suggested, to permit a logically consistent social welfare function to be derived. These conditions are beyond intuitive interpretation; quite generally, they stipulate a certain homogeneity of preferences.

Any alternative may be characterised by various attributes or dimensions. When deciding between various road projects, voters may consider the width, the pavement, the consequences on environment, etc.

In the case of multi-dimensional alternatives, the necessary and sufficient conditions just mentioned are extremely restrictive. Black's requirement of single-peakedness corresponds to complete unanimity of individual preferences in the multi-dimensional space. Even a small inhomogeneity of individual preferences can lead to logically inconsistent outcomes. If the Impossibility Theorem is to be circumvented, individual preferences must be arranged in a completely symmetrical way around the equilibrium point; even a small deviation can again lead to paradoxical social decisions.

This theorem suggests that in reality cyclical majorities may *always* be possible. Modern research has shown that voting outcomes extend over the whole admissible area (and are not restricted to the set of Pareto-optimal solutions). This means that the Impossibility Theorem implies grave contradictions between preliminary outcomes (i.e. outcomes that may be beaten by other alternatives) with respect to *content*.

Preference intensities and vote-trading

If the Arrow condition of the Independence of Irrelevant Alternatives is abandoned, a number of possibilities arise for getting around inconsistent results. It is presumed that individuals have the capacity to undertake an overall comparison among all the alternatives. The comparison between only two alternatives (binary voting method) considered so far is substituted by other voting procedures which permit the expression of relative preference intensities.

With *point voting*, a given total number of points may be distributed among the various alternatives. The voters may express the relative evaluation of the alternatives by correspondingly allotting points in the voting process. With this procedure, however, a new problem arises. The more strongly individuals are able to make their preference intensities known by voting, the stronger is the incentive for *strategic voting*: an individual can attempt to influence the voting outcome by *not* voting according to his true preferences; the collective decision will in general be biased, and the social welfare function derived cannot be considered to be a sensible aggregation of individual preferences.

Strategic voting is most pronounced with point voting but arises with *all* (non-dictatorial) voting procedures. Individual voters may have an incentive to misrepresent their true preferences under all voting rules. Voters can reveal varying preference intensities which they attach to the alternatives available even in the case of simple majority voting by *vote-trading*, whereby they attempt to get through their most preferred alternative(s) by renouncing their less preferred alternative(s).

Vote-trading may be demonstrated with a simple example. Three voters (I, II, III) are assumed to attach (in terms of cardinal numbers) the following subjective utility gain (positive number) or utility loss (negative number) if the two alternatives (A, B) are accepted, compared with the *status quo*.

Voters	Alternatives	
	A	B
I	−3	−3
II	8	−3
III	−3	8

If the alternatives are decided upon in isolation, voters I and III vote against A, and voters I and II against B, so that both alternatives are rejected.

The majority with less intensive preferences tyrannises the minority with more intensive preferences, however. The rejection of alternative A denies voter II a utility gain of + 8, and the rejection of alternative B denies voter III a utility gain of +8. Compared to this, the majority winners would lose only 3 utility units each when alternative A is accepted, and the same holds for alternative B. If, however, voter II votes for alternative B on the condition that voter III votes for A, *both* alternatives are *accepted*: voters II and III vote for A as well as for B, and voter I with his negative vote is now in the minority as regards each alternative. If it is assumed possible to add the utility numbers used, the numerical example shows that collective utility rises owing to the vote-trade: after vote-trading, the net utility amounts to $-3+8-3= +2$, for each alternative.

Vote-trading always increases the utility of the voters participating (because otherwise they would not undertake it). The voter(s) *not* participating in the trade, on the other hand, suffer a utility loss (in the example, -3 for each alternative). The joint action of vote-traders imposes a negative external effect on other voters. This negative externality can be larger than the utility gain of the vote-traders. Such an outcome pertains in the following example.

Voters	Alternatives	
	A	B
I	-3	-3
II	5	-3
III	-3	5

The same vote-trade between voters II and III is *individually* rational, total utility of all the voters falls with the acceptance of alternatives A and B. Compared with the *status quo*, after vote-trading, two voters lose 3 units each and one voter wins 5 units, thus totalling $-3+5-3= -2$, for each alternative.

It can be proved that in case of *multiple* vote-trading between the voters, each individual voter is worse off *after* the trading operation than before. This possible conflict between individual rationality and collective welfare may be called the *paradox of vote-trading*.

Vote-trading does not allow us to get around the voting paradox. On the contrary: those constellations of preference intensities making vote-trades advantageous to the voters also fulfil the preconditions for the appearance of cyclical majorities. To illustrate this proposition, the utility numbers for alternatives A and B used in the first table resulting in vote-trading are augmented by an alternative C.

Voters	Utility of alternatives			Preference orderings
	A	B	C	
I	-3	-3	-4	A=B>C
II	8	-3	9	C>A>B
III	-3	8	-2	B>C>A

Included in the table are the individual preference orderings corresponding to the subjective utility appraisals. Voter II for example prefers alternative C to alternative A because C gives him 9 and A only 8 utility units. A is preferred to B by voter II because C gives him a utility loss of 3 units. His preference order thus is C>A>B.

With simple majority voting among the three voters, A and B receive the same number of votes ($1\frac{1}{2}$), and C is beaten by B by 2:1 votes.

For reasons of transitivity, it follows that alternative A is preferred to alternative C; a direct vote between A and C results, however, in a 2:1 majority for alternative C. When vote-trading is possible, contradictory social decisions are possible.

MAJORITIES, UNANIMITY AND THE CONSTITUTION

The single majority is without any doubt the most widely used voting rule. It is usually adopted without any further thought; often it is considered to be the essence of democratic decision.

This preference for simple majority rule (in contrast to a qualified majority such as two-thirds or three-quarters) may be shown to be justified: simple majority is the *only* decision-making rule meeting the four (apparently sensible) requirements:

(1) Unrestricted Domain of individual preferences;
(2) the social decision is independent of what preferences particular individuals have (Anonymity);
(3) the social decision is also independent of the labelling of alternatives (Neutrality); e.g., the *status quo* has no special position compared with new alternatives;
(4) when alternatives x and y in the preference order of *some* voter are reversed, *ceteris paribus*, the social decision is to change in the same direction if the collectivity was indifferent before (Positive Reaction).

As may be seen intuitively, the four requirements are *special cases* of Arrow conditions (1)–(4); i.e., the Impossibility Theorem applies also to the (simple) majority rule.

Apart from this axiomatic approach, voting rules may also be analysed from the point of view of an individual. The question now is, what decision-making rule will a rational individual choose in the 'natural state'? As a representative individual is considered, it follows that his reflections also apply to society as a whole. This individualistic approach forms the logical counterpart of an organic conception of the state. The state is exclusively looked at as an *instrument* for fulfilling collective wants revealed by individuals.

The most consequent approach in this direction is due to Buchanan and Tullock. They attempt to fix the 'optimal' division between private and collective action. The larger the percentage share of voters who must agree to collective action, the smaller is the danger for a representative individual to be harmed by the fact that the collective action may be against his wishes (external costs). In the case of the unanimity rule each individual can, if he wants to, block social action. In addition to external costs, the individual has 'decision-making costs' because it is more and more difficult to agree on joint action the larger the required share of consenters. A voter's optimum is where the sum of external and decision-making costs is minimal. Simple majority rule turns out to be quite arbitrary; the decision-making rule should be different for each kind of collective action.

In deciding which type of majority should be required for which joint activity, the basic decision-making rule about the choice of specific decision-making rules is to be fixed in the constitution. According to Buchanan and Tullock, it must be taken by unanimous vote. This is the only way of preventing the majority of voters from fixing a decision-making rule on the constitutional level in such a way that the remainder of the voters (minority) always has to carry the external costs of collective action.

Instead of all the individuals, it is also possible to consider a group of men forming the constituents who in the natural state have complete knowledge about future objective possibilities and subjective preferences but who know neither the identity of individuals in the various positions nor their preferences. Thus they know *how many* will be rich and poor, progressive and conservative, etc., but they do not know *who* will be what (including themselves). With this kind of 'perfect' information, which disregards the interests of any *particular* individual, it is possible to reach complete unanimity in the constitutional assembly.

Buchanan and Tullock's approach has been criticised for many reasons. It has been argued that a decision-making rule determines not only the group able to bring about a change but at the same time the group able to prevent change. The unanimity rule asymmetrically gives a great advantage to those who, with the help of the vote, are able to maintain an initial position in which they benefit at the cost of the rest of society. Simple majority rule has the optimal property of minimising the tyranny of a conservative minority without, at the same time, giving another minority the power to bring about changes.

This idea has been formulated more precisely. It starts from the assumption that no individual knows the future preferences of the other voters and that, therefore, he is inclined to think that he accepts and refutes them with equal probability. Simple majority under this assumption is optimal in the sense that the number of cases in which the representative individual does not agree with society's decision is minimised. It is, however, presumed implicitly that the consequences of the two cases in which the individual is in the minority are valued equally; namely (1) if the individual is *for* an action but the majority refutes it and (2) if the individual is *against* an action but the majority adopts it.

The difference between the requirement of unanimity advanced by Buchanan and Tullock and the proposition of optimality of simple majority rule is due to the fact that implicitly different conditions are looked at. Buchanan and Tullock consider the case in which the collective supply of a good or service is under debate. A reasonable requirement on the constitutional level is that the supply should take place only if a Pareto-optimal condition is reached (see also the Arrow conditions). This means that each individual expects to be better off; i.e., the decision must be taken unanimously.

The other position is concerned with the possibility of changes in the distribution of income and wealth by collective action. The Pareto Criterion is in this case inapplicable because those who lose income or wealth are negatively affected. As it is unknown on the constitutional level in which direction the proposals for redistribution go, and whether one belongs to the rich or the poor, simple majority is optimal for this situation as it minimises the number of issues in which the individual is overruled by the majority.

MEDIAN VOTER AND PUBLIC GOODS

The ideas discussed so far in this chapter have been on an abstract level. Some aspects of the theory of voting may also be applied practically.

In votes under simple majority rule, the *median voter*, being 'in the centre' of the voters' range of preferences, plays a decisive role: it is he who may convert a minority into a majority.

This property may be demonstrated by a simple example of the demand for a public good where the individuals must agree on a joint volume of consumption. The three voters I, II and III must determine the volume by simple majority vote, but they have different evaluations of this public good. Voter I has little interest in the consumption of this good and correspondingly has a low marginal willingness to pay for all quantities. Voter II is assumed to have a medium and voter III to have a high marginal evaluation. These curves of marginal evaluation (or marginal willingness to pay, MWP) are shown at the top part of Figure 6.3. In contrast to private goods – where each consumer is confronted with the same price but where he can choose the quantity he likes – in the case of public goods 'prices' are individually fixed for each consumer: these are the taxes to be paid in connection with the supply of the good. If the three voters constitute the whole population, and the analysis is restricted to one good, total production cost of the public good must be covered in one way or another by corresponding tax receipts. The sum of tax shares of consumers/voters – in our case t_I, t_{II}, t_{III} – must thus be equal to the marginal production cost of the public good (MC); i.e., $t_I + t_{II} + t_{III} = MC$. In the upper part of Figure 6.3 it is assumed for simplicity that the tax shares are fixed *a priori* and that they are constant. The tax share of the first voter, t_I, is assumed to be medium, that of the second voter, t_{II}, to be small, and that of the third voter, t_{III}, to be large.

The upper half of Figure 6.3 shows the individual optima of the three voters ($0_I, 0_{II}, 0_{III}$); they are determined by the equality of marginal utility (or marginal willingness to pay) and marginal cost

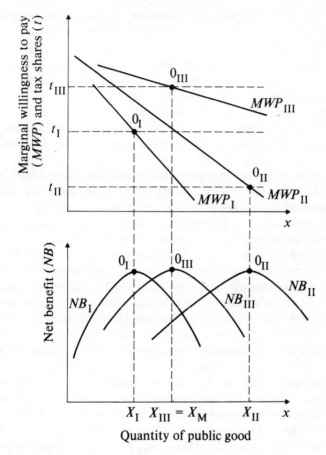

FIG. 6.3. *The role of the median voter* (X_M)

(or marginal tax share). The first voter experiences a positive *net* marginal utility up to quantity X_I and beyond that point a negative *net* marginal utility. Total net benefit (*NB*), which results from a comparison of total benefit from consumption with the tax costs to be paid is shown in the bottom part of Figure 6.3. (The height of these curves is without importance, as no interpersonal comparison of utility is undertaken.) The quantity of the public good most desired by the second and third voters is X_{II} and X_{III}, respectively.

To reach a collective decision about the amount of the public good to be supplied a step-wise procedure is used. Assume that quantity X_{III} is the point of departure. A motion to produce a *smaller* quantity, e.g. X_I, is supported by the first voter only; the second and third voter have a higher net utility with a larger public good supply. The same happens to all motions proposing a supply below X_{III} because in each case the first voter is in the minority. All motions proposing an increase of collective supply *beyond* X_{III} will be supported by the second voter but rejected by the majority. For both the first and the third voter a supply larger than X_{III} means a loss of net utility in comparison with quantity X_{III}. The proposition to produce quantity X_{III} is the only one to reach a majority. The third voter is in this case the *median voter* because his optimal demand for the public good is in the centre (median) of all voters. This median voter's demand is indicated by X_M in the figure. The median voter is the one who turns a minority into a majority.

This analysis may be extended to any number of voters. As may be seen from the lower part of Figure 6.3, the (here continual) preferences of individuals are *single-peaked* (so that the paradox of voting does not occur). It should, however, be noted that voters I and II are not satisfied with the outcome of the election in so far as they are not in their individual optimum given the tax prices. They will make an effort to change tax prices, and will be successful if this decision also is taken by simple majority rule. Yet another distribution of the tax burden can win yet another majority, etc.; i.e., the variability of the tax system leads to instability.

Simple majority decisions lead to Pareto-optimal outcomes (if single decisions are considered) only by chance. Majority rule thus is no procedure guaranteeing a (potential) improvement for each individual. A Pareto-optimal supply of a public good requires equality of the *sum* of the individual marginal willingness to pay (ΣMWP) with marginal cost of production. Figure 6.4 extends Figure 6.3 by these two curves. The requirement that marginal cost (MC) be covered by the individual tax shares ($t_I + t_{II} + t_{III} = MC$) is again taken into account.

The Pareto-optimal supply X_{PO} in this example is larger than the supply X_M agreed upon by majority rule. At the Pareto-optimal quantity *net* marginal utility of voter III is already negative and he will, therefore, vote against this larger quantity.

The supply decided upon by majority rule and the Pareto-optimal supply are equal if the median voter is in his individual optimum at the Pareto-optimal quantity. The condition of equality of marginal

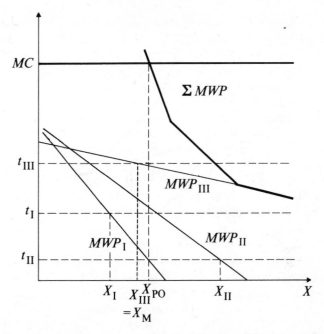

Fig. 6.4. *Simple majority outcome (median) and Pareto-optimum*

benefit and marginal cost is met for the median voter if *his* tax price corresponds to his marginal willingness to pay. To secure a Pareto-optimal supply of public goods it has been suggested that the tax share of *each* voter is equated to his marginal willingness to pay (at the Pareto-optimal quantity). This so-called Lindahl solution is illustrated in Figure 6.5.

The requirement of equality of tax price and willingness to pay for *each single* voter goes further than necessary to reach a Pareto-optimal allocation, but it has the advantage that the majority decision corresponds to the individual optimum of all the voters. Given tax prices, no voter has an incentive to revise the decision.

The median voter model can be used for forecasting voting outcomes as well as for empirical analysis. This model is particularly useful in the study of the determinants of public expenditures according to various categories (such as for schooling, police protection, roads, etc.).

So far, in analogy with traditional econometric estimation procedure, *average* income and tax burden have been used as explana-

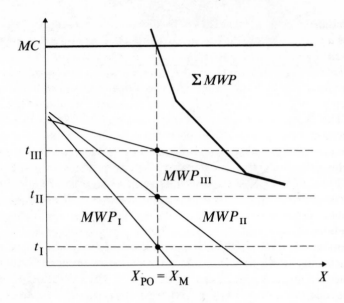

Fig. 6.5. *The Lindahl solution*

tory variables. No theoretical justification has been given for this. Empirical research on communities with direct majority voting over public expenditures has shown, however, that the use of data relating to the *median voter* (in particular his income and tax price) yields superior results.

Outlook

The search for the possibility of aggregating individual preferences without contradiction is completed. Minor refinements of the ideas presented are, of course, still possible. The discussion has, however, become sterile. A comparison between rising research input and poor results suggests that further research in this direction makes little sense. Important insights can rather be won by considering *new aspects*. For example, discussion, which forms an important element in each decision-making process, could be included. In most cases preferences are probably not invariably given and may, therefore, not simply be aggregated by voting. The process of decision-making itself shapes individual preferences, and therefore has a decisive effect on the outcome reached by collective action. Even if an abstract formulation of the aggregation problem is justified for some questions, allowing for the effect of discussion and bargaining on individual preferences would constitute an important step towards decision-making processes found in reality.

The analysis of which problems are actually subject to explicit decision-making is another important aspect. Again, it is not directly relevant to the fundamental aggregation problem, but it helps us to understand and improve decisions made in real life.

The examination of the problems of the *constitution* and of *decision-making rules*, in particular in connection with the theory of public goods, is much more stimulating than the general theory of preference aggregation. The scientific discussion between the proponents of the concept of constitutional contract (in particular Buchanan, Rawls and Nozick) and other views is presently taking place. Interesting conclusions emerge about the definition of 'justice' and therefore about income distribution, as well as about the limits of the public and private sector.

Worthwhile developments are meanwhile taking place in the search for *new decision-making mechanisms*. Quite original is a two-step procedure. In the first step individual random vectors indicating the preferences of the voters among the various alternatives are aggregated to social probabilities; in the second step the 'winning' alternative is chosen with the help of a random mechanism (e.g. an urn). This procedure allows preference intensities to be taken into account and circumvents the paradox of voting.

Another new voting procedure attempts to solve the fundamental problem of preference misrepresentation by strategic voting. The attempt to ask citizens to reveal their true preferences with the help of surveys or by voting usually does not work. The possibility of acting as a free rider to get around contributing to the cost of producing a public good has been pointed out before. The procedure that serves to induce individuals to reveal their true preferences is based on the following idea. Each voter has to pay a tax corresponding to the *negative external effect* that he imposes on the other voters. Such negative externalities arise if the other voters accept a project because the sum of their willingness to pay (counted in monetary units), or of utility – after taking account of the cost – is positive, but the voter in question turns the total sum of utility negative by stating *his* negative marginal willingness to pay. A negative externality also exists if the negative utility sum from a project revealed by the other voters is turned positive when the positive willingness to pay of the voter in question is added. If the voters that reveal a marginal willingness to pay that is able to change the voting result based on the total willingness to pay have, in addition, to pay a tax amounting to the negative external effect imposed upon the others, they will act in their best interest by revealing their *true* willingness to pay in the political process. This voting procedure guarantees that society accepts Pareto-optimal proposals only.

Such ideas are certainly stimulating. Research should not, however, be limited to the analysis of the axiomatic properties. It is also necessary to study the possibilities and limits of *applying* such voting procedures. Questions of legitimacy and implementation of such decision-making rules, as well as possible historical experiences, must also be subject to research.

LITERATURE

There exist some survey articles on public choice with many references to the literature:

Dennis C. Mueller, 'Public Choice: A Survey'. *Journal of Economic Literature*, 14 (1976)

Bruno S. Frey, 'Entwicklung und Stand der Neuen Politischen Ökonomie'. In: H. P. Widmaier (ed.), *Politische Ökonomie im Wohlfahrtsstaat*. Fischer-Athenäum, Frankfurt, 1974.

A good textbook on public choice, which is especially devoted to the relationship of various decision-making rules to the price system, is

Peter Bernholz, *Grundlagen der Politischen Ökonomie*, Volumes I and II. Mohr (Siebeck), Tübingen, 1972 and 1974.

A more strongly mathematically orientated textbook, which also deals with the underlying rationality assumptions, is

William H. Riker and Peter C. Ordeshook, *An Introduction to Positive Political Theory*. Prentice Hall, Englewood Cliffs, 1973.

The game-theoretic contribution, particularly to the theory of voting, is well developed in

Steven J. Brams, *Game Theory and Politics*. Free Press, New York, 1975.

Also to be noted is

Albert Breton, *The Economic Theory of Representative Government*. Aldine, Chicago, 1974.

A comparison between the economic and sociological approaches to political science is provided in

Brian M. Barry, *Sociologists, Economists and Democracy*. Collier-Macmillan, London, 1970.

Some important articles on public choice are collected in

Bruce M. Russet (ed.), *Economic Theories of International Politics*. Markham, Chicago, 1968.

Precursors of the economic theory of politics are

Knut Wicksell, *Finanztheoretische Untersuchungen*. Gustav Fischer, Jena, 1896

Joseph A. Schumpeter, *Capitalism, Socialism and Democracy*. Harper and Row, New York, 1942.

Among the classics, count

Kenneth J. Arrow, *Social Choice and Individual Values*. (2nd ed.) Wiley, New York, 1963

Duncan Black, *The Theory of Committees and Elections*. Cambridge University Press, 1958

Anthony Downs, *Economic Theory of Democracy*. Harper and Row, New York, 1957

James M. Buchanan and Gordon Tullock, *The Calculus of Consent. Logical Foundations of Constitutional Democracy*. University of Michigan Press, Ann Arbor, 1962

Mancur Olson, *The Logic of Collective Action: Public Goods and the Theory of Groups*. Harvard University Press, Cambridge, Mass., 1965.

Black's book contains a nice description of the origin of the theory of voting, a derivation of the median voter model and the requirement of single-peakedness to get around the voting paradox.

The general theory of preference aggregation is excellently developed in

Amartya K. Sen, *Collective Choice and Social Welfare*. Oliver and Boyd, Edinburgh and London, 1970.

An equally good presentation is by

Michael Taylor, 'The Theory of Collective Choice'. In F. I. Greenstein and N. W. Polsby (eds), *Macropolitical Theory* (Handbook of Political Science, 3), Addison-Wesley, New York, 1975.

A short book treatment is given by

David J. Mayston, *The Idea of Social Choice*. Macmillan, London, 1974.

The illustration of the voting paradox with the fable by Aesop is taken from

William A. Fischel, 'Aesop's Paradox: The Classical Critique of Democratic Processes'. *Journal of Political Economy*, 80 (1972).

Table 6.1 in the text, giving the probabilities of finding no majority winner, is taken from

Richard G. Niemi and Harold F. Weisberg, 'A Mathematical Solution for the Probability of the Paradox of Voting'. *Behavioral Science*, 13 (1968), p. 322.

Two most important articles on preference aggregation under simple majority are

Charles R. Plott, 'A Notion of Equilibrium and its Possibility under Majority Rule'. *American Economic Review*, 57 (1967)

Gerald H. Kramer, 'On a Class of Equilibrium Conditions for Majority Rule'. *Econometrica*, 41 (1973).

The discussion of vote-trading follows Mueller's survey article quoted above. The relationship between vote-trading and the paradox of voting is discussed by

Peter Bernholz, 'Logrolling, Arrow Paradox, and Decision Rules – A Generalization'. *Kyklos*, 27 (1974).

The four conditions to derive simple majority rule are due to

Kenneth O. May, 'A Set of Independent, Necessary and Sufficient Conditions for Majority Decision'. *Econometrica*, 20 (1952).

The proof of the optimality of this rule from the standpoint of the individual is by

Douglas W. Rae, 'Decision Rules and Individual Values in Collective Choice'. *American Political Science Review*, 63 (1969).

The conditions for Pareto-optimal supply of public goods have been derived by

Paul A. Samuelson, 'The Pure Theory of Public Expenditure'. *Review of Economics and Statistics*, 36 (1954).

A comparison between the models using median and average data to explain public expenditures for a Swiss canton has been undertaken by

Werner W. Pommerehne and Bruno S. Frey, 'Two Approaches to Estimating Public Expenditures'. *Public Finance Quarterly*, 4 (1976).

The two-step decision procedure has been suggested by

Michael Intriligator, 'A Probabilistic Model of Social Choice'. *Review of Economic Studies*, 41 (1973).

The voting procedure employing a tax on negative externalities imposed is developed in

Nicholas Tideman and Gordon Tullock, 'A New and Superior Process for Making Social Choices'. *Journal of Political Economy*, 84 (1976).

7.   A Modern Theory of Institutions

The survey on public choice has so far considered only the conditions under which individual preferences may be aggregated in order to reach a consistent social decision or to construct a complete social welfare function. This aggregation can be taken to be an element of every political process, and is, therefore, independent of institutions. In the last chapter the properties of particular decision-making rules such as unanimity or simple majority have already been discussed and it has been shown that even in the general framework of the median voter model it is possible to derive inferences about reality.

Government and political parties, as well as interest groups and the civil service, have not been discussed so far. Public choice deals intensively with these institutions and is able to give interesting insights into their behaviour. In contrast with traditional economic theory, which concentrates on the working of the price system and is largely abstracted from institutions, public choice may be viewed as a *modern theory of institutions*. The first section of this chapter deals with political parties, the second with the government, the third with interest groups and the last one with the civil service.

POLITICAL PARTIES

Up to now, traditional economics assumes that state and government maximise society's welfare. Particularly in the theory of (quantitative) economic policy (and elsewhere), an *explicit* social welfare function is subsumed and its optimum is derived taking account of various side-constraints. In contrast with this view, public choice regards the state and government as institutions composed of *selfish individuals*; it completely breaks with the organic conception of the state. The somewhat naïve but still widely accepted notion is rejected that all is well if the government takes over an activity that is subject to market failure. When state decision-makers act, 'private' benefits and costs (i.e. those internal to an organisation) may considerably deviate from social benefits and costs. A tendency therefore arises to act in a socially non-optimal, or biased, way. The government's take-over of an activity leads to an optimal outcome only if specific conditions are fulfilled. The most important requirement is that parties compete for votes on a perfectly functioning political market. The analogy to the model of the economic market is obvious: in place of profit-maximising entrepreneurs there are vote-maximising politicians, and in place of consumers there are voters, who also maximise their own utility. In the political area the same behavioural assumptions are made as in the economic area. The results of the two models also correspond with each other: Adam Smith's fundamental vision that the *selfish* behaviour of market participants (under specific conditions) leads to a *social* optimum also obtains in the political 'market'. The maximisation of general welfare does not depend on the goodwill but rather on the pursuit of the private advantage, by economic and political actors.

The basic model

The economic theory of political party competition has been worked out by Downs. His analysis has shaped subsequent research. The idea of spatial party competition – in which the space is interpreted not geographically but rather as the positions of party programmes – has been formalised for the case of two competing parties, and the model is now completed. The central relationship analysed between voter preferences and the policy undertaken by the government has never been treated adequately in traditional political science.

In the simplest case the position of individual voters is marked on a (unified) scale (in Figure 7.1, i.e. from 'left' to 'right'). Curve D gives the density of various ideological views, i.e. the percentage of voters having a particular political view. In the figure it is assumed that most voters have a 'medium' position and that there are only a

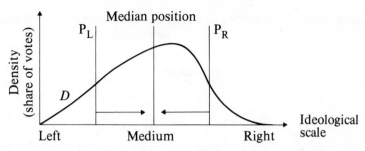

FIG. 7.1. *The position of political parties and the distribution of voters' preferences*

few voters with extreme left and right views. Each voter casts his vote for the party that is nearest to his own position.

It is assumed that there exist a 'left-wing' party (P_L) and a 'right-wing' party (P_R) which both want to form the government and which must, therefore, attempt to get as many votes as possible. The positions of the two parties shown in the figure are not at equilibrium. The party of the left for example would win votes if it suggested and put into action a programme that was more in the middle of the vote distribution; many voters who were closer to the right-wing party would then vote for the other party, which has moved closer to their own views owing to the change of position. Voters with a position left of the previous position of the left-wing party will go on voting for it because it is still closer to their view than the right-wing party.

The same applies to the right-wing party. It can win votes from the opposing party by moving towards the centre. A position of equilibrium is reached only when both parties are in the *median* of the voter distribution. The parties then no longer differ with respect to their ideological position, and each one of them receives the same number of votes and thus has the same chance of getting to power.

The same outcome results if the voters assemble around more than one position, as shown in Figure 7.2. Each of the two parties can expect an increase in votes by moving more closely to the competing party's position. In equilibrium the two parties advance a programme in the median of the vote distribution, a position which, however, in that case is preferred by only a few voters.

The two-party model can be generalised from one ideological scale to various *different policy dimensions*. In this case it is likely that no position exists that could not be beaten by a position taken by the competing party, owing to the Impossibility Theorem.

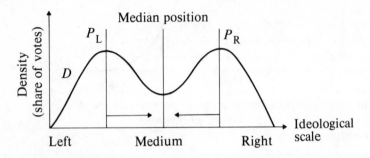

FIG. 7.2. *Case of bimodal voter distribution*

In a *state of equilibrium* the following results obtain for the standard model of two-party competition.

(1) The two parties offer identical programmes in the centre (median) of the vote distribution. Chance decides which one is in power at a certain time and puts the programme into action. The same results thus follow as with simple majority rule: each party must reach a majority to win the elections; by his decision, the median voter has the possibility of securing the election victory for one of the two parties.
(2) There is no 'exploitation' of voters because party competition erases every monopoly profit of the party in power.
(3) Equilibrium is Pareto-optimal. If any voter could improve his position without damaging another voter, one of the two parties could offer a corresponding programme and would thereby win at least an additional vote at the cost of the other party. The result corresponds with the policy that an ideal 'benevolent dictator' would undertake. When tax prices and therefore distributional aspects are introduced there arise problems, however. As has been mentioned in the consideration of the median voter model, unstable majorities may appear when tax prices are variable.
(4) A rational voter participates in the election only if the party programmes differ. As they are identical in equilibrium, perfect democracy is characterised by complete vote abstention. High vote participation is of no value as such – quite contrary to the traditional view. What matters is that voters react strongly if one or both parties deviate(s) from the optimum, i.e. in disequilibrium situations.

The conclusion that in equilibrium of perfect democracy voting participation is zero is not drawn by all authors because some assume that the electorate internalises voting as a duty. This may well be so, but such an assumption is ad hoc, stands outside the rational-economic model and is close to a tautology.

The four central results of the model clearly show the interpretation of 'competition' given by economic theory. In practical politics and in practical science one speaks of 'competition' when two parties have programmes strongly differing from each other. According to economic theory, in such a situation there is no 'competition' as neither of the two parties attempts to win votes at the cost of the other party by proposing a programme nearer to the opponent's programme.

Extensions of the basic model

Besides taking account of various programme dimensions, the model of party competition has been extended in various directions.

(1) *Modification of behavioural assumptions.* With a given number of voters Downs' hypothesis of vote maximisation follows from the superior goal of politicians and parties to get to, or stay in, power. If vote abstention is taken into account, parties must attempt to maximise a vote majority. If a party is considered a coalition of various groups under a leader, the goal may be the 'minimisation of majority', because then the party leader can give the highest rewards (in the form of power, prestige or income) to each one of the groups supporting him.

(2) *Extension of the number of competing parties.* The study of the competition of more than two parties creates grave problems because of the possibility of coalitions. The direct selection of the government from the election outcome as assumed in the basic model applies today to Anglo-Saxon but not to continental European countries, where governments are usually composed of a coalition of various parties. If coalitions are excluded, a uniform distribution of voters over the ideological scale is assumed, and if strategic voting is disregarded, more than two competing parties assemble around the two extremes while the central positions are occupied by one party each. For the special case of three parties there exists no equilibrium. Both results do not correspond with the constellations found in reality.

(3) *Dynamic elements.* There are few satisfactory attempts to analyse the temporal process of party competition. One theoretical study comes to the conclusion that, owing to the paradox of voting, the party in government changes at *each* election, but this contradicts the experience in democratic countries (e.g. in Scandinavia).

(4) *Protest.* In the model of perfect party competition it is advantageous for each party to move to the centre of the programme scale. The voters holding extreme political views are put in a worse position. They nevertheless support the same party because it is still nearer to their own optimum than the other party. Though the threat of exit thus is of no

effect, voters at the extremes have a specifically political means of stating their preferences, namely by protesting. They can mobilise so far unused resources to influence 'their' party; they can increase their participation in the political process; and can thereby make it impossible for the party to move to the centre.

Application of the model of party competition

Elements of this competitive view of the political process have been used to analyse various aspects of politico-economic interaction. A summary must suffice here.

Taking account of uncertainty and differential information, the size of budget resulting from a democracy has been studied. There is a tendency for a government to prefer producers (i.e. the recipients of income of any kind, including employees) at the cost of consumers. For each group an increase in their own income is felt more strongly, while price increases damage a large number of consumer–voters only imperceptibly. In a similar direction goes the attempt to introduce various economic sectors into the model of political competition. Under plausible assumptions it may be shown that the government prefers sectors with slow growth and low capital intensity. The model of party competition may also be applied to problems of nationalism. Other applications refer to trade unions, foreign trade, social policy, natural environment and finally personal and intertemporal income distribution. In the last application various generations are distinguished which are either consumers only (the pensioners and the young), or are at the same time producers (the active or employable generations). Depending on the assumptions about the number of people in these groups as well as their political participation, it is possible to derive interesting conclusions about inter-generational income transfers.

Evaluation of the model

The 'pure' theory of party competition has been formalised in a more and more axiomatic way in analogy with the theory of perfect economic competition. The models become increasingly abstract. The goal of the formal analyses consists of the derivation of the exact conditions under which an equilibrium of party competition exists and a Pareto-optimal or welfare-maximising outcome is reached.

The *pure* theory of party competition has been developed so far that probably not much additional knowledge will be gained in the future. Progress requires the introduction of new elements. This is particularly obvious in the case of competition between more than two parties, for which case formal analysis does not find any satisfactory solution. This result suggests that the few building blocks of the model are insufficient in view of the complex problem. The model must be enriched, for which purpose a number of theoretical and empirical analyses from other parts of public choice are available, such as the study of coalition formation or the relationship between the distribution of parliamentary seats and the selection of the party coming into power. The 'applied' models of party competition may also provide fruitful new elements, e.g. the difference in information among voters and the combination of interest groups and economic sectors. The inclusion of such aspects considerably changes the theory of party competition and combines it with other parts of political economy.

GOVERNMENT BEHAVIOUR

Various hypotheses may be advanced concerning the behaviour of a party or a coalition already in power. It is implicitly assumed that there is no perfect competition with the opposition party for votes, but that the government has to a certain extent the *possibility of pursuing its own interests*. The more leeway the government has to pursue its own goals, the more strongly its behaviour deviates from the one analysed in the theory of perfect party competition.

Vote maximisation at election time

The government is subject to election approval in time intervals only, in most countries every three to five years. In many countries the government may also be overthrown by the parliament within a legislative period. This possibility is particularly relevant when no party commands a clear majority. But even in this case general elections constitute a decisive break.

In many democracies the party in power has a parliamentary majority, or the government is formed by a stable coalition of various parties which together have a majority. In this case public choice often assumes that the government maximises votes at election time. The government pursues a policy resulting in the largest number of votes at the forthcoming election even if before the election (and after winning the election) it is less popular with the voters. To a large extent optimal policy depends on the speed with which voters forget the government's achievement over the course of the legislative period. If the voters are orientated towards the present, they evaluate the government exclusively according to its achievements shortly before the election. In that case the government makes an effort to create the preconditions during the first years of an election period in order that in the election year a policy may be undertaken that will have particular attraction to voters. If the voters have a memory extending further into the past, the government cannot afford to pursue such an extreme policy but must make an effort to offer a policy favourable to voters also in the years previous to elections. Empirical research indicates that voters discount the past quite quickly.

Utility maximisation subject to constraints

The discretionary scope of government is the larger the less intensive competition among the parties is. If the government does not pursue a vote-maximising policy it need not necessarily lose the election. It can undertake a policy corresponding with its own preferences as long as it receives the required number of votes at election time. This behavioural hypothesis of utility maximisation subject to a re-election constraint corresponds with the basic premises of public choice, which assumes rational behaviour also in politics. As the members of government have a limited time horizon, the government tries to realise its utility as soon as possible; i.e., future utility is discounted. The content of the utility function is not determined *a priori*. It is realistic to assume that government politicians have an interest in putting their ideological programme into practice, and besides that in increasing their prestige and possibly even their income. Re-election is a necessary requirement for the achievement of these goals; a party out of power cannot make its ideological views become reality.

Besides the political re-election constraint, there is a number of other influences restricting the scope of government action. The administrative constraint indicates that government is forced to seek and maintain the support of the civil service. It can put into practice its goals contained in the utility function only if the civil service accepts its plans or at least does not oppose them. The government is also restricted by economic constraints: it cannot expand expenditures too far compared with receipts but is bound by the budget constraint. In many countries the scope for decision is further narrowed by the need to keep the balance of payments in equilibrium.

In this theoretical approach government behaviour is described by a complex dynamic maximisation problem subject to a number of constraints. The government seeks to approach the optimal solution by a simplified decision procedure taking the political re-election constraint as the starting point. As long as the government confidently expects to be re-elected, it can afford to follow its ideological predilections even if they are popular with part of the electorate only. If, on the other hand, the government believes that its re-election is in danger, it must concentrate all effort on devising actions popular with the voters.

Coalition against the voters

The government has the largest leeway if political parties do not compete with each other but, on the contrary, form a coalition against the voters. Such a situation is unlikely on the government level as it is unstable: it pays for a single party to leave the coalition by proposing a programme popular with the voters, to thereby win the election, to form the government without the previous coalition parties, and to appropriate all the utility from governing. As an extreme opposite to the usual vote-maximisation model this behavioural assumption is not without interest, particularly because some aspects of such an anti-voter coalition may be found in reality.

INTEREST GROUPS

In public choice, groups are studied in connection with the supply of public goods. As an exclusion from the consumption of such goods is impossible or too costly, no rational individual will join a group that supplies such a good. If it is (realistically) assumed that the cost of making and maintaining a corresponding agreement rises with the number of members, the following non-exclusive conditions for the existence of economic and political groups may be derived.

(1) The group must be so small that a mutual dependence and therefore a pressure for conforming behaviour arises which may lead to an agreement for joint supply.

(2) The public good must be supplied jointly with private goods available only to the paying members of the coalition.

According to this approach trade unions, for example, may exist only if they can force workers to join them (e.g. by closed shops) because the wage increases achieved as a rule benefit *all* workers employed in the corresponding sector. Trade unions may also exist because they offer social facilities similar to clubs. This analysis is in opposition to Marx, who saw the decisive factor for group formation in 'class consciousness'.

The demands of those parts of the population to which none of the three conditions for effective organisation applies need not necessarily remain unheeded. Enterprising politicians may take up their wishes and try to mobilise these sectors of the population to cast their votes for them so that an advantage results for both sides.

From condition (1) given above an unconventional result may be deduced, namely a tendency for the exploitation of the large by the small. Within an organisation the large members may derive such great benefit from the public good that they are ready to supply it on their own. The bargaining position of the large is, therefore, relatively weak, with the result that they carry a more than proportional share of cost. This theory has empirically been verified at the example of NATO, to which the United States contributes a share of the cost far out of its proportion. The medium and small nations are fully aware that they benefit from the public 'good' of defence even if they pay little or nothing of the cost. The economic theory of groups has also been supported empirically by trade union formation in Germany, the United States and the United Kingdom.

Goods which within a group of members have a certain degree of publicness, but from the consumption of which non-members may be excluded, enable the group size resulting from rational behaviour of individuals to be determined. The total cost of supplying a good with these characteristics is assumed to be shared equally among all the group members. With a good that is purely

public *within* the group, utility is (by definition) independent of the
size of group, while the cost per member continuously falls as the
group size increases. The individuals are, therefore, interested in a
group size as large as possible.

A group whose utility falls with rising membership after a certain
point owing to congestion has the individual utility and cost curves
shown in Figure 7.3. Up to group size $\bar{M}$, the utility of each member
increases. The optimal group size, however, is not yet reached
because cost is falling more quickly than benefit per member. Only
group size M^* maximises net benefit per member; the member's
marginal benefit corresponds with his marginal cost at this point.
Examples of such benefit and cost curves can often be found in
clubs: with too few members, the advantages of club life are not
fully reaped (e.g. in tennis clubs there is too small a choice of
partners), whereas with too many members there is mutual congestion (the tennis courts are so much in demand that there are
uncomfortable waiting times).

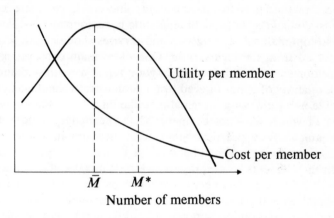

FIG. 7.3. *Determination of optimal group size*

BUREAUCRACY

The last section was concerned with the possibility of organising
groups and with their external influence. This section considers the
internal functioning of existing organisations. At the centre of atten-

tion is the civil service; it is, however, well known that bureaucracy in large (private) enterprises differs only slightly. The importance of bureaucracy in today's world is well illustrated by the great success of popular books, such as those by C. Northcote Parkinson.

The economic approach starts with the assumption that bureaucrats attempt to maximise their own utility and are not directly interested in the official goals of the organisation. The real goal of bureaucrats is to increase their own power, prestige and security – and also their income. These are all elements closely linked with the hierarchical position in a formal organisation. Bureaucrats having scruples with respect to their own behaviour are at a disadvantage in such an organisation because they deny themselves certain possibilities for action.

This approach to the analysis of bureaucracy has some analogy with the price system. A member of a bureaucracy is subject to similar constraints to those in the market: he deals with persons who indicate to him whether they are harmed or benefited by his decision. He thus gets to know benefits and costs; i.e. there is an 'invisible hand' governing bureaucratic behaviour.

No 'optimal' supply of goods and services should, however, be expected from the civil service. One of its main concerns is the development and maintenance of good relations with parliament. The quantity of goods offered by an administrative unit is an indivisible unit (and not a marginal unit like on a private market) the cost of which may not be higher than the budget allocated by parliament. As a practical behavioural assumption, *budget maximisation* may be assumed because the budget is highly correlated with the elements in a representative bureaucrat's utility function discussed above. The services offered by the civil service correspond with the demand revealed by parliament: if demand is large, a corresponding amount of public goods and services is offered until it is completely satisfied. If, on the other hand, it is small, only that quantity is offered that uses up the budget. In both cases supply is too large: marginal cost is larger than marginal benefit.

It is difficult to analyse bureaucratic behaviour as evidenced by the (mostly politological) studies on the development of public expenditure undertaken so far. This approach, called 'policy output studies', is quite untheoretical and attempts to explain a maximal share of the variance with the help of regression analysis. In this respect the attempt to use 'incrementalism' as the basis for testing the budget process constitutes only a small progress. The differences in the amount to which the budget is marginally expanded as in time or between administrative units may not be explained by this approach. First attempts to offer a theoretical explanation capable of accounting for such aspects have been undertaken within public choice.

LITERATURE

A simple discussion on the formal model of party competition is given by
Otto A. Davis, Melvin Hinich and Peter C. Ordeshook, 'An Expository Development of a Mathematical Model of the Electoral Process'. *American Political Science Review*, 64 (1970).

An extended development is also to be found in Chapters 11 and 12 of the textbook by Riker and Ordeshook already quoted at the end of the previous chapter. In particular, the proof of Pareto-optimality of two-party competition is given. An excellent discussion of the problems arising with variable tax prices is in the second volume of the book by Bernholz, also quoted in the previous chapter. An analysis of competition among more than two parties is provided by
Reinhart Selten, 'Anwendungen der Spieltheorie auf die politische Wissenschaft'. In H. Maier *et al.* (eds), *Politik und Wissenschaft*. Beck, Munich, 1971.

The abstract model of dynamic party competition mentioned is by
Gerald H. Kramer, 'A Dynamical Model of Political Equilibrium'. *Journal of Economic Theory* (forthcoming).

Coalition formation between parties is discussed by (among others)
Michael Taylor, 'On the Theory of Government Coalition Formation'. *British Journal of Political Science*, 2 (1972).

The effect of a differential level of information about taxes and public expenditures is analysed in
Anthony Downs, 'Why the Government Budget is Too Small in a Democracy'. *World Politics*, 12 (1960).

Various assumptions about government behaviour – in particular utility maximisation subject to constraints – are discussed in
Bruno S. Frey and Lawrence J. Lau, 'Towards a Mathematical Model of Government Behaviour'. *Zeitschrift für Nationalökonomie*, 28 (1968).

The economic theory of groups is due to Olson. The possibility of improving one's position by voluntarily agreeing to be forced to contribute to the supply of public goods is developed in
William J. Baumol, *Welfare Economics and the Theory of the State*. (2nd ed), Bell and Sons, London, 1965.

The theory of optimal group size is due to
James M. Buchanan, 'An Economic Theory of Groups'. *Economica*, 33 (1965).
The fundamental contributions to the economic theory of bureaucracy are by
Anthony Downs, *Inside Bureaucracy*. Little, Boston, 1967
Gordon Tullock, *The Politics of Bureaucracy*. Public Affairs Press, Washington, 1965
William Niskanen, *Bureaucracy and Representative Government*. Aldine-Atherton, Chicago/New York, 1971.
Downs and Tullock deal with the internal relationship within bureaucracy; Niskanen looks at the external relationship in analogy to the theory of the firm.
'Policy output research' is represented by (among others)
Ira Sharkansky, *Policy Analysis in Political Science*. Markham, Chicago, 1970.

Part III

HOW CAN EVOLUTIONARY DEVELOPMENTS ARISE?

The next two parts of this book are devoted to the application of
political economy to practical problems. The approach used is the
new political economy that results from an integration of elements
of public choice with unorthodox political economy. The weight of
the two elements is variable; the third part relies more on unorthodox political economy, the fourth part more on public choice.
The unifying theme of the two parts lies in the analysis of the
government's behaviour under different economic and political
conditions. The government is seen to have a central position in
society; its effort to stay in power is one of the basic characteristics
of politico-economic systems. The possibilities and limits to the
government's actions are strongly determined by economic factors
which have an effect upon the political sector. The government can
influence the economy in various ways. This *mutual interdependence of the economy and the polity* may take various forms,
depending on what specific assumptions are made concerning the
economic and political system.

In this third part the emphasis lies upon the *dynamic development*
of the economy and the polity. Chapter 8 deals with the demand for,
and supply of, infrastructure; Chapter 9 with the demand and
supply of public goods. Infrastructure and public goods have many
aspects in common. In the case of infrastructure its character of an
investment into the stock of the economy's real capital is stressed; in
the case of public goods their character as consumer goods is considered. The analysis shows that the dynamic development of infrastructure and public goods is inseparably combined with cyclical

movements which are induced by the interactions between the economy and the polity. This evolutionary view of economic development, which deviates fundamentally from the equilibrium (steady-state) growth concept of traditional economics, constitutes a step towards the political economy of the Unorthodox.

8. Fluctuations in Economic Growth

Economic growth cannot be explained solely by economic factors. This statement is obvious from even a casual look at reality. It is accepted by laymen and politicians, and also by economists.

Modern growth theory, however, expounds a completely different picture. Political factors are completely missing in growth models. Not only is the influence of voters, interest groups and political parties disregarded, but also institutions such as the government and the civil service are missing.

Most economists would concede that the inclusion of political factors in the analysis of economic growth is important. They hold the view, however, that it is not up to the economists to take account of such factors; such a task should be left to political scientists. This view cannot be upheld, as has become clear from the preceding chapters.

THE INFLUENCE OF INFRASTRUCTURE ON PRIVATE CAPITAL AND TECHNICAL PROGRESS

The infrastructure comprises a wide area: traffic, energy, education, research, health, natural environment, defence, administration, police and justice. These sectors are extensively interpreted below; at the centre of attention is the *investment aspect*.

In connection with economic growth two factors are particularly important.

(1) The infrastructure is for the most part a public good, the use of which is open to everybody.
(2) The infrastructure is mostly supplied by the *state*. The quality and distribution of the infrastructure are politically determined and do not obey the rationale of the price system.

While the first property is taken into account by some authors, the second – and more important – aspect has been paid almost no attention in connection with economic growth.

The size and productivity of *private entrepreneurial* capital are not independent of the infrastructure. The relationship between the two is a decisive determinant of the middle- and long-run growth of the economy. The connection is quite simple: if the infrastructure exists in abundance (over-capacity), growth of national income and of productivity is high; if the infrastructure is scarce (under-capacity), there is a tendency for slow growth and a small increase in productivity. Excess and lack of infrastructure must always be seen in relation to the level of economic activity. The decisive relationship is thus between *changes in flows* (growth rates of the economy) and *stocks* (infrastructure). It would, however, be possible also to describe the relationships between production (and underlying private capital) and infrastructure in terms of flow. In an economy expanding rapidly and having sufficient infrastructure, an implicit flow of services goes as input into the production process. If this input factor were taken into account in the aggregate production function, the weight of overall capital would be considerably higher, and correspondingly the importance of technical progress would diminish.

In empirical research the concept of use of the infrastructure is difficult to apply. It is a characteristic, particularly of natural infrastructure, that its use largely proceeds unnoted and its importance is realised only later. Only if for example air and water are so much polluted that production and consumption are severely hampered, is it recognised that one is dealing with infrastructural goods. The infrastructure thus does not comprise areas defined once for all: its extent and importance change in the course of economic growth.

During the time of an excess supply of the infrastructure relative to the demand at the existing national income, the average overall capital coefficient is high (owing to the heavy weight of the infrastructure) while the marginal capital coefficient for private entrepreneurial investment is low. The rate of return on investment in the market sector is high, which constitutes another factor for the rapid growth of national income. On the other hand, where there is a shortage of infrastructure the overall capital coefficient is low while the marginal capital coefficient for private market investment is high.

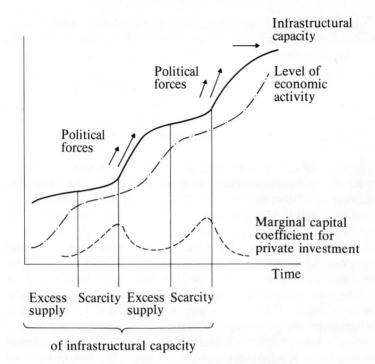

Fig. 8.1. *Infrastructural capacity and economic activity*

Figure 8.1 shows the relationship between infrastructural capacity (the reasons for its sudden upward jumps are discussed later), the level of economic activity, and the marginal capital coefficient for private market investment.

In traditional growth theory it is suggested that technical progress may be directly increased by increasing current expenditure for research and education. According to the present view, technical progress is a pure reflection of the relationship between infrastructural capacity and corresponding economic activity. A large supply of infrastructure enables the economy to grow rapidly with a small input of labour and private capital – which is nothing other than rapid productivity growth and high technical progress. This effect is *ceteris paribus* the higher
– the larger the stock of educational and research capital, and
– the larger the stock of other infrastructural capital.

An increase in *current* expenditure for education can be expected to have only a long-run effect on the rate of growth, namely when summed investments appreciably increase the stock of education beyond the initial level. The same applies to other types of infra-structural investment.

POLITICAL FACTORS IN ECONOMIC GROWTH

The importance of politics for economic growth stems directly from the fact that the supply of the infrastructure is determined not by the market but almost exclusively by the political decision-making process. The following discussion applies to democratic countries in which voters and interest groups may have an influence upon government decisions. The influence of short-run activity of the government on the economy (particularly demand management) is not considered here.

The political process of the supply of the infrastructure is determined mainly by the interaction of the political parties (one of which forms the government) and the voters (who elect the party in power at regular intervals). Interest groups affect both government and voters. It is assumed that two large political parties oppose each other. Their only goal is *vote maximisation*, in order to stay in power as long as possible. No party has a preconceived ideological view; rather, those problems are included in the programme that are expected to attract the greatest number of voters. The party winning the election forms the government. It acts rationally by increasing expenditures as long as the gain in votes (by citizens benefited) is just balanced by the loss of votes (by citizens experiencing higher taxes and/or price increases.

Each voter casts his vote for that party promising him the largest utility. The voter knows that the winning party will make an effort to fulfil its election promises because otherwise it would lose the voters' confidence and undermine its chances for re-election. The interest of voters in economic problems changes during the growth process. Usually, each voter is most concerned with his interests as a producer (supplier of goods, capital, labour or services). In periods of increasing infrastructural scarcity the voter will, however, also be interested in problems of the infrastructure as they affect his production and consumption possibilities.

The degree of information available to voters is of great importance for a realistic analysis of the political process. If a party in power can depend on the fact that voters are not very well informed about the benefits and costs of its actions, it will pursue no programme in which the costs are obvious (e.g. some types of tax increases) while the benefits are hidden (e.g. by arising in only the far future). It should again be noted that the voters' degree of information differs according to the specific economic situation. If, for example, the infrastructure is in abundance, the voters are only poorly informed about it by the mass media; if the infrastructure is in scarce supply the flow of information about it increases, owing to its growing newsworthiness to the mass media.

THE GROWTH PROCESS

Over-supply of infrastructure

Assume a situation with an abundance of infrastructure. This excess supply of infrastructural capacity causes a low capital coefficient and high profitability of private investment, resulting in rapid economic growth. At the same time labour productivity and technical change are high, enabling a rapid rise of real wages and of consumption. Owing to the high growth rates of output and productivity, the rate of inflation is small.

The party in government has no reason for undertaking additional infrastructural outlays since there is currently no demand for it and voters do not recognise expenditures with benefits only in the distant future. The opposition party has no influence on current infrastructural investment. It sees no reason for stressing the topic of infrastructure in its programme as long as there is no shortage troubling the voters.

Shortage of infrastructure

The more that infrastructural capacity is employed by producers and consumers, the more the capital coefficient for market investments rises, as it is no longer easily possible to increase production simply by using the infrastructure. Some services that before were offered by public infrastructure must now be financed and produced by private enterprise if these are to expand further. Generally, there is a substitution of public capital by private capital. A decisive expansion of the infrastructure therefore cannot be achieved, as a large part of the infrastructure has the property of a public good and because certain infrastructural goods can be supplied by the state only.

The rise in the capital coefficient for private market investments leads to a fall in the rate of growth in the economy if the rate of investment does not strongly go up (for which there is no reason). Technical progress diminishes so that real wages and consumption increase more slowly. Under these conditions it is unlikely that the rate of inflation will increase.

The lack of infrastructure has mostly negative consequences. Are there forces in the political area able to get the economy out of this unpleasant situation by bringing about the necessary supply of infrastructure?

The *party in power* is in a difficult position, as it is accused of not having done its duty (if it has been in power over some period) by letting this shortage of infrastructure arise. In spite of this, the governing party will not change its infrastructural policy, for the following reasons.

(1) In the past (in which there was an abundance of infrastructure) the policy of neglecting the infrastructural issue proved successful. No institution is happy to change a position that has proved advantageous in the past. At the same time, there is the danger that a change of direction of infrastructural policy may irritate the up-to-now faithful voters and project the image that the party is going back on its election promises. Furthermore, there is the unwillingness of the civil service (on which every government has to rely) to alter expenditure shares once accepted as justified.

(2) The party in government will deny that the economy has already reached its infrastructural capacity, as it would thereby admit that it has not fulfilled its duty.

(3) The party in government knows that to a large extent infrastructural investments bear their fruit only in the distant future while the taxes and price increases necessary to finance them are felt by the voters immediately. It is, therefore, more advantageous to the government to pursue a policy of immediate vote gain, particularly by handing out subsidies to specific groups in the population.

The *opposition party*, on the other hand, will concentrate all its effort and propaganda on the infrastructural topic and promise large infrastructural investments in their programme. They will do so for the following reasons.

(1) The shortage of infrastructure is recognised by the consumer–voters and will therefore be used by the opposition to demonstrate the government's bad record. The opposition party will make every effort to inform the voters about these shortcomings.
(2) The opposition party loses little or nothing by pursuing a new line of policy as it is not in power, anyway. Moreover, it has no ideology to defend on the ground that it has proved successful in the past.
(3) The party not in power can make more promises regarding the development of the infrastructure without having to bear the same unpopular consequences (higher taxes, lower expenditures in other sectors or higher prices), as its statements are discounted by the uncertainty of its winning the next election.
(4) The opposition party can possibly induce producer interest groups to give money to its election fund by promising improvements in the infrastructure. The relative improvement in the financial position increases the opposition party's election chances.

The *voters* as consumers also directly realise the lack of infrastructure, e.g. bad air and dirty water, insufficient police protection, etc. Equally important is the increased degree of information on the infrastructure brought about by the propaganda of the opposition party and producer interest groups. It is thus not true that there is propaganda only for private consumer goods, as claimed by Galbraith. Moreover, voters are negatively affected by the general worsening of economic conditions caused by the lack of infrastructure.

For these reasons, some voters will decide to vote for the opposition instead of for the party in government. The party in power will then lose votes and (possibly) the election.

Re-establishment of excess supply of infrastructure

The demand for an expansion in the infrastructure leading to a change of government is the result of political forces arising in a democracy owing to the lack of infrastructure. These political forces tend to bring about a supply of infrastructure in excess of prospective demand, for the following reasons.

(1) The propaganda for infrastructural expansion undertaken by the former opposition party and interest groups leads to a change in the conventional wisdom (that only private capital matters) of the voters and public officials. Changes of well-established beliefs often lead to an

overly strong reaction in the opposite direction, i.e. to an over-estimation of the importance of the infrastructure for economic growth. It is probable that certain infrastructural projects are undertaken by the government only to meet the demands of voters and interest groups. As the extent of an increase in the infrastructure is the result of a complicated political process, there is no guarantee that the amount of infrastructure additionally demanded really corresponds with the requirements of the economy. Uniform growth is impossible because there is either *no* interest in infrastructure (when there is abundance) or a *very strong* interest in it (when there is a shortage); i.e., the economy must necessarily expand in cycles.

(2) When the political forces caused by a shortage of infrastructure arise, considerable time passes before the infrastructural capacity deemed necessary is built up, for the following reasons.

(a) There must be a change of government before a decisive change of infrastructural policy takes place.

(b) Infrastructure has a long gestation period and can be supplied only in large units (indivisibility).

During the whole period of build-up the political forces are active, as the increase of infrastructural capacity is not yet felt. This leads to a capacity increase in excess of current requirements. The point of departure is reached again; the precondition for further cyclical expansion is established.

THE POLITICAL ECONOMY OF GROWTH

The result of the process discussed may be summarised in the following way.

(1) For political reasons it is impossible to bring about the 'correct' supply of infrastructural capacity. There is, therefore, no possibility for uniform economic growth. Trend and cycle of economic activity are simultaneously determined.

(2) When infrastructure is scarce the political forces arising lead to a strong tendency for a change of government.

(3) This change of government leads to an increase of infrastructural supply in excess of current requirements.

(4) The larger the shortage of infrastructure, the stronger the compensating political forces. The political forces arising are weak only if the shortage of infrastructure is small and chronical, the subsequent change of government is delayed, and the overall majority of the party in power is small.

This theory considers the process of economic growth as the

result of an inseparable interplay of economic and political forces. The circle between the two forces is closed: economic conditions bring about the decisive political forces, which in turn have a large influence on economic conditions.

The theory is optimistic: general equilibrium theory proves that the economy ideally reaches a (Pareto) optimum owing to the *automatic forces of the market mechanism.* These optimality conditions, derived for a stationary economy, do not necessarily apply to a growing economy. It seems to follow that in a non-stationary economy there is no reliance on automatic forces. This discussion suggests that in an expanding economy *political forces* accompany the market mechanism, which in a democracy remove disequilibria and set the preconditions for long-term development.

LITERATURE

Modern (neoclassical) growth theory is excellently presented in
   Robert M. Solow, *Growth Theory: An Exposition.* Clarendon Press, Oxford, 1970.
   Empirical aspects of economic development are discussed in
   Simon Kuznets, *Modern Economic Growth.* Yale University Press, New Haven, 1966.
   Fundamental contributions to the theory of infrastructure are discussed in
   Jacques Stohler, 'Zur rationalen Planung der Infrastruktur'. *Konjunkturpolitik*, II (1965)
   René L. Frey, *Infrastruktur.* Mohr (Siebeck) Tübingen (2nd ed.), 1972.

9. Cycles in the Demand and Supply of Public Goods

The last chapter developed a political theory of economic growth and argued that in modern economies, in which infrastructural investment plays a large role, it does not proceed uniformly but rather in cycles. The decisive change from a shortage to an over-supply of the infrastructure is accompanied by a change in government.

This chapter considers the temporal sequence of the demand for, and supply of, infrastructural goods. In contrast to the last chapter, the consumption rather than the investment aspect is stressed. The emphasis is on the characteristic properties of public goods, on the separation between consumption and contribution to the cost of supply, and on the impossibility to measure its output objectively. *Time lags* play an important part; the result is again that a uniform supply of public goods is impossible and that there are necessarily marked fluctuations.

THE NEED FOR A DYNAMIC THEORY

Existing public goods theory is completely stationary, and is concerned mainly with deriving the conditions for an efficient equilibrium. It has come to the unequivocal conclusion that – except under very special circumstances – *the market* is not able to bring about a Pareto-optimal supply of public goods: no rational consumer is prepared to reveal his preferences for a public good on the market and to contribute to the costs of its supply.

The *theory of political competition* concludes on the other hand that, in the case of two political parties, a Pareto-optimal supply *is* achieved. This result applies to *all* goods supplied through the political process, irrespective of whether the goods are private or public. As has already been mentioned, the model of political competition is faced with considerable problems. With two parties, unstable outcomes may result if tax prices and therefore income distribution are varied. With three political parties no equilibrium exists, and with four or more parties very curious results follow. It is therefore questionable whether this approach may be maintained – at least in its present formulation.

The theory of public goods is in an awkward position. The inefficiency of the price system is proved; but the possibilities and limits of the political system – not to speak of other decision-making mechanisms – are little known.

A *dynamic* theory of public goods does not yet exist. The temporal element is, however, very marked in this area, owing to the interaction of economic and political forces.

POINTS OF DEPARTURE FOR A DYNAMIC THEORY

A dynamic analysis requires three realistic assumptions:

(1) the supply of public goods is a time-consuming process;
(2) the *benefits* of public goods consumption are completely separated from the *contribution to the costs* of its supply; the exclusion principle is not applied; this separation becomes obvious to its full extent only when viewed as a process of demand and supply;
(3) the benefit from public goods cannot be measured objectively; the willingness to pay is revealed insufficiently or not at all.

The assumptions concerning the non-exclusion principle and non-revelation of preferences belong to the definitional properties of public goods; no additional psychological and sociological factors are introduced.

For all economic goods the following phases of demand and supply may usefully be distinguished:

(1) rise of disequilibrium;
(2) articulation of demand;
(3) reaction to demand;
(4) supply of the good.

It is contended that these phases occur differently in the case of public goods as compared with private goods. The reason lies in the fact that in the case of public goods the possibility of consumption is divorced from payment, i.e. from the contribution to the costs of supply, while in the case of private goods a good may be used only if the corresponding price (in perfect competition the marginal production cost) is paid. The cycle in private goods is usually almost invisible, though there are cases in which it can be observed: in West Germany, for example, there were in the 1950s successive 'waves' for food, clothing, housing and travelling.

To analyse such phases in the case of public goods a model is constructed containing an economic and a political sector. Instead of the two traditional decision-making units (households and firms), the present analysis considers four:

(1) consumer–voters,
(2) government,
(3) civil service,
(4) producers.

The opposition party and interest groups play a somewhat less important role. Each of the four groups mentioned above is assumed to maximise its own utility. In the case of the government this boils down to vote maximisation, in the case of the civil service to the maximum increase of influence, prestige and income, which in turn are closely related to the size of the budget allocated.

PHASES IN THE PUBLIC GOODS CYCLE

The typical time phases connected with the demand and supply of public goods are discussed in turn.

A disequilibrium arises

A disequilibrium in consumption, or – more generally – a dissatisfaction with the presently consumed bundle of goods, may arise for a great many reasons: income may have risen; relative prices may have changed; new goods (or goods of better quality) may have been introduced; or preferences may have shifted. Consumers then wish to adjust the structure and the level of their consumption.

With private goods, each consumer can turn to the market, which (in general) will quickly respond to the increase in demand by inducing producers to supply more. With public goods there exists no market in which these wants can be made known. At best there are substitutes for the services of the public good desired. However, these are mostly available to higher income groups and at (strongly) increasing costs only. If for example environmental quality deteriorates, relatively few families are able to move to unaffected areas.

Not only consumers, but also producers feel the disequilibrium. Production costs rise in those sectors in which public goods are employed as input factors to a particularly strong extent.

Demand is articulated

To express their wishes, consumer–voters and producers must turn to the *political system*. They must make it clear to the government that an increase in the supply of the public good concerned will yield the government large benefits and that a refusal of their demands would cost it votes and possibly lead to an election defeat.

It is the characteristic of this phase that

(1) *benefits are stressed* while costs are neglected; therefore
(2) there is practically *unanimity* about the desirability of supplying the public good; and therefore
(3) there is an *over-demand* for the public good (compared with a situation in which marginal costs are considered). This preference revelation may be called 'political demand'.

The reason for the over-demand lies in the neglect of costs. Costs are not relevant for any group in this phase because their distribution is yet undecided. Everyone hopes that the others will pay. Even if there is some experience about the method of financing the public good, each group knows that there are a great many ways of shifting costs between individuals and groups. Cost distribution is undecided because the public good may be financed by ordinary taxes, by supplementary credits or simply by printing some more money. Cost distribution is also strongly affected by the general state of the economy, because tax-shifting strongly depends on aggregate demand. For these reasons the groups demanding public goods are at this stage little concerned with the cost aspect.

Figure 9.1 shows Pareto-optimal demand X^* (determined by the equality of the summed curves of individual marginal willingness to

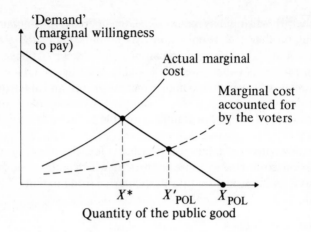

FIG. 9.1. *Pareto-optimal demand and political demand*

pay with marginal cost) and political demand. Disregarding cost completely, political demand is X_{POL}; if only part of the cost is considered it is X'_{POL}.

What matters is that in this phase *political demand* is larger than Pareto-optimal demand. With a political revelation of the demand for public goods (under the assumptions made), the opposite result obtains from that on a market. It is wrong to infer that the demand revealed for public goods is generally too small (compared with true demand); on the contrary, in politics demand is usually overstated.

The government reacts

The demand expressed in the political sphere cannot be overlooked by the government, especially as it is so unanimous. However, it may be that the government is fixed on another political line, and that it fears it will confuse its voters by changing its policy. This problem is less likely to arise if (unlike the case of infrastructural shortage discussed in the last chapter) the increase in supply demanded concerns *specific* public goods only. The government may, however, evaluate the situation incorrectly, or may simply make a mistake and not react to the political demand. In that case it will lose votes, and the opposition will finally take over with a programme including a promise to increase the supply of the public good concerned.

The old or new government, committed to fulfil the political demand, is forced to become active. In view of its goal of vote maximisation, it will undertake actions that are clearly visible to the electorate, and that can be undertaken in short time.

These criteria can be met most easily on the *input side* of the public goods policy. Thus plans, programmes and laws will be formulated and institutions will be founded (e.g. new ministries established). The erection of buildings takes longer but their opening can be made to catch the public's eye. The prime concern of the government thus does not lie with the *output side* of the public goods policy, i.e. with actual supply, because that side is difficult to measure and takes considerable time to implement.

Supply of the public good

The activities of the government lead to costs that slowly are felt by the electorate and interest groups. The tax burden rises, new duties are introduced, and real income (or at least its rate of growth) falls if the cost is financed by expanding money supply. Political discussion is reversed compared with phase two: the *cost of providing the public good is now dominant, while benefits are played down.* The reason lies in the fact that (expected) benefits from public goods supply can be enjoyed by everyone, regardless of whether he has contributed to cost. Every individual and group in society attempts to shift the cost of government activity upon someone else, even if his *net* benefit from the provision of the public good is positive. Every group tries to evade contributing to cost by pretending that it benefits only little or even nothing from the public good. This is possible in so far as an objective measurement of public goods benefits is difficult.

At this stage of the cycle conflicts between and within socioeconomic groups arise. The question of the *distribution* of benefits will be raised, and some consumer–voters will begin to realise that they benefit comparatively little from the public good.

For producers the moment has come to make their influence felt. Their pressure groups inform the government about the negative consequences for price stability and employment if they are forced to pay (part of) the cost of providing the public good. Like the various consumer groups, they can claim that they benefit little from the public good without running the danger of being proved wrong.

The government gains the (possibly sad) experience that, when it comes to cost, the unanimous support for the public goods policy rapidly vanishes and even turns into hostility. To keep in power it will adopt a strategy in which

(1) (partial) successes of its public goods policy are stressed: this will have little effect, as in this phase each group is interested only in minimising its cost share;

(2) politically well organised and powerful interest groups are effectively excluded from the contribution to cost: the government can do this in a number of different ways, starting from specific exemptions from laws in which the distribution of cost is determined, to hidden or open subsidies to compensate for cost;

(3) expenditures for the public good are reduced (at least compared with other outlays).

THE OUTCOME

The government's strategy leads to a decrease in the supply of the public good compared with initial 'political' demand and corresponding plans and programmes. There are no forces, however, that drive the politico-economic system to Pareto-optimal supply, as *net benefits* are not articulated in any phase of the cycle. Actual supply depends on the effects of the actions undertaken by the government in the third phase, and on the degree of autonomy of the civil service, which tries to prevent a decrease in outlays.

EXAMPLES OF PUBLIC GOODS CYCLES

In Western industrial countries several waves of demand for, and supply of, public goods can be identified since World War II:

(1) aid to developing countries;
(2) economic growth;
(3) education, research and development, and health;
(4) environment.

All these 'goods' have consumption characteristics (i.e. give immediate utility), and the exclusion principle is not applied. In so far as aid to developing countries gives utility to the *donors*, it benefits all industrialised countries. Economic growth has the properties of a public consumption good in so far as an increase in investment raises the welfare of *all* members of the present generation that have an interest in the well-being of future generations. Utility thus is independent of the contribution to cost, in this case consisting of a sacrifice of present consumption. Education is partly a public good because a certain level of education is a prerequisite for democracy; it eases the communication between the members of society and makes deviant behaviour (e.g. crime) less likely. The public goods properties of environment need not be stressed, they are a classic case in point.

The cycles of the demand and supply of these materially quite different public goods all have the same sequence. A disequilibrium arises leading to political demands and to a reaction from the government. When the problem of financing the expenditures arises a reaction sets in leading to activities even in the opposite direction.

The enthusiasm for growth of the early 1960s decreased, for example, when the required cost in terms of present consumption sacrifice, and especially in terms of the negative effects on natural environment, became apparent. The resulting enthusiasm for environmental controls led to demands for zero growth. But the enthusiasm for such controls decreased when the individual taxpayers and various groups realised that the environmental policy demanded required sizeable personal sacrifices. Especially for the lower income groups, such an extreme policy would have meant too high a sacrifice of private consumption expenditures.

At this stage, for the first time, the distributional consequences have been discussed, e.g. that the higher income groups benefit particularly strongly from an improvement of environmental conditions. The enthusiasm for education, finally, which was established in the mid-1960s and which led to an extraordinary growth of outlays on the input side, has been scaled down by the strongly felt increase in the tax burden of a large share of the population.

LITERATURE

A good introduction to the theory of public goods is given by

James M. Buchanan, *Demand and Supply of Public Goods*. Markham, Chicago, 1968.

A somewhat more formal discussion of public goods and externalities is given in the first part of the textbook

William J. Baumol and Wallace E. Oates, *The Theory of Environmental Policy*. Prentice Hall, Englewood Cliffs, 1975.

The theory of public goods is moreover covered in all modern textbooks on public finance. All these approaches are, however, static, and are concerned mainly with the normative properties for Pareto-optimality.

Part IV

HOW CAN POLITICO-ECONOMIC INTERDEPENDENCE BE MEASURED EMPIRICALLY?

The concluding chapters of this book deal mainly with empirical analysis. This aspect is neglected in all variants of political economy, including public choice. It is shown that it is insufficient to look only at statistical time series (or cross-sections): the relationship must be studied with the help of an explicit theoretical model, from which quantitative hypotheses can be derived and empirically tested.

An area in which empirical research in political economy seems to be most fruitful is *politico-economic models*. Their goal lies in the quantitative study of the mutual interdependence between the economy and the polity.

The influences going from the economy to the political sector, and the influences going from the polity to the economic sector, are considered to be of equal importance. At the centre of analysis is the *government* (as in Part III). It is assumed that it intends to maximise votes, subject to various constraints such as the need to secure re-election, through instruments of economic policy. The *voters* evaluate the government's performance according to the state of the economy; they determine through their vote whether or not the government should change. The interaction between the government and the voters, as well as the dynamic structure of the economy, can lead to *political business cycles.* Various reasons for such politically induced cycles are distinguished. The idea of the government willingly producing business cycles is diametrically opposed to the notion inherent in traditional economics, according to which the government dutifully makes an effort to avoid business cycles.

The tenth chapter considers politico-economic models limited to a *special sector of the economy*; Chapter 11 deals with politico-economic models covering the *whole economy*; in the closing chapter a *politometric* estimate of a simple politico-economic model is presented using econometric methods. The estimates refer to very recent periods of the United States and the United Kingdom.

10. The Interrelationship between the Economy and the Polity

Public choice analyses the way in which voters' preferences are fulfilled in the political process. This view is exemplified by the models of party competition (discussed in Chapter 7), which are concerned with the relationship between voters' preferences and party programmes. This interdependence is shown in Figure 10.1 in a simplified way. The upper link shows the programmes presented to the voters by the two parties, A and B. The voters evaluate them according to their preferences and decide between the two parties by casting their vote.

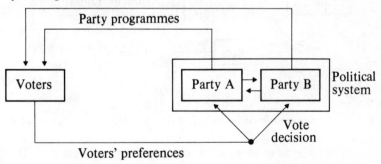

FIG. 10.1. *Schematic representation of the model of party competition*

Voters' preferences extend over a great many areas, including economic issues such as income growth or the rate of inflation. It may be seen from the figure that the model of party competition does not make an explicit assumption about the relationship between economic variables and the possibility of influencing them by political action. It is only assumed that the programmes proposed are economically feasible and that they can be put into action by the winning party.

Politico-economic models intend to introduce the economic sector explicitly and to analyse how the state of the economy influences voters' preferences and thereby the evaluation of the parties, and in what way the government in turn influences the state of the economy. The emphasis is on the *interdependence between the economic and political sectors*. The competition between the parties is of less importance; the government is at the centre of political action. It must, however, be on guard against being thrown out of power by the opposition party (or parties).

The basic idea of a politico-economic model is given in Figure 10.2. The lower loop shows how the state of the economy – represented by a number of economic variables – influences the voters

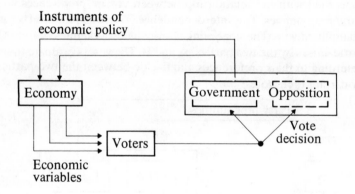

FIG. 10.2. *Schematic representation of a politico-economic model*

and motivates them to vote for or against the government. The government is able to influence the economic sector with the help of instruments of economic policy. This relationship is shown in the lower loop.

The *partial* politico-economic models discussed in this chapter consider a particular part of the economy. The relationship between unemployment and inflation is taken as an example; it has so far received most attention in research. Partial politico-economic models have also been applied to the choice between current and future consumption, i.e. to the intertemporal allocation problem.

UNEMPLOYMENT AND INFLATION

The point of departure is the conception that there is a negative relationship (a so-called 'Phillips Curve') between the level of unemployment and the rise in the general price level. The higher unemployment, the lower the rate of increase in wages and (with a given development of labour productivity) in prices. The rate of inflation, moreover, depends on the *expected* rate of inflation, because trade unions want to maintain the real income of their members and will, therefore, ask for higher wage increases when the future price level is expected to be higher. Expected price rises depend on the experience in the recent past: inflation expectations will rise when actual price rises have been underestimated in the past (and conversely).

It follows from these empirically confirmed assumptions that there is in the *long run* a stable trade-off between unemployment and inflation, but that in the *short run* the relation shifts because inflation expectations change. The long-run Phillips Curve is characterised by the fact that expected inflation has been completely adjusted to actual inflation. Figure 10.3 shows two such short-run curves (S_1, S_2) and the steeper long-run Phillips Curve (L).

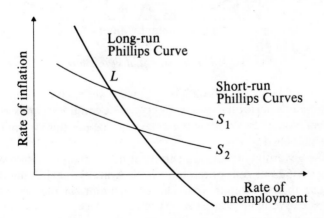

FIG. 10.3. *Short- and long-run trade-offs between unemployment and inflation*

VOTER AND GOVERNMENT BEHAVIOUR

Voters evaluate unemployment and inflation negatively. They would prefer a state of full employment and stable prices. It is realistic to assume – and it will be empirically shown in the next chapter – that the voters hold the government responsible for unemployment and inflation. The higher the rates of unemployment and inflation, the smaller will be the government's share of the votes.

Figure 10.4 shows three curves of constant vote share of the government; the nearer these iso-vote curves are to the origin (i.e. the lower the unemployment rate), the higher is the government's share of the votes.

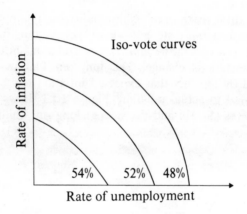

FIG. 10.4. *Curves of equal vote share*

In the following discussion it is assumed that the voters judge the government's performance only by economic conditions in the *election year*. As will be shown in the following chapter, this assumption is not unrealistic.

If the government wants to survive it must attain a certain vote share, say 52 per cent of the total vote. A utility-maximising government in the election year chooses a point on the short-run Phillips Curve lying *inside* (or *on*) this 52 per cent vote curve.

Figure 10.5a gives a situation in which the government loses the election because it finds it impossible to reach this area. At a given time the government can make a choice only on a particular short-

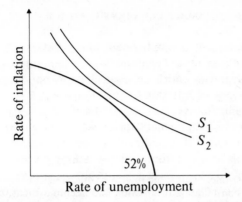

FIG. 10.5a. *Situation in which the government is defeated at elections*

run Phillips Curve; in Figures 10.5a and 10.5b this is indicated by S_2. In Figure 10.5b the government at election time can gain more votes than is necessary for re-election; the hatched area AB shows the discretionary room within which it can choose a utility-maximising position.

A vote-maximising government will lose the election in the situation shown in Figure 10.5a; in the situation shown by Figure 10.5b it will choose point V^* in which the short-run Phillips Curve S_2 is tangent to the iso-vote curve nearest to the origin (in the figure it is assumed to be 54 per cent of the total vote). Each other point yields fewer votes.

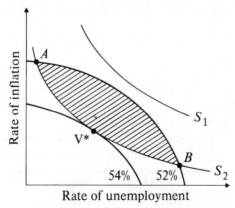

FIG. 10.5b. *Situation with discretionary room and vote maximum of the government*

CONSTANT AND VARIABLE GOVERNMENT POLICY

The combination of unemployment and inflation chosen on the short-run Phillips Curve at election time (S_2 in Figure 10.5b) cannot be upheld over the entire ensuing election period because the induced changes of inflation expectations lead to a shift of the short-run Phillips Curve. A *long-run equilibrium*, in which the rates of inflation and unemployment are constant over time (the so-called steady state), exists if a point on the long-run Phillips Curve is achieved. This long-run equilibrium is taking place if

(1) the government (for some reason or other) has the goal of fixing an unchanged constellation of inflation and unemployment; or
(2) there are exogenous restrictions forcing the government to undertake such a constant policy, e.g. because there are no appropriate policy instruments to influence the economy in the short run; or
(3) the election periods are very long (more exactly: infinitely long).

Steady-state equilibrium

A *vote-maximising* government pursuing an economic policy of constant unemployment and inflation will select a point in which the long-run Phillips Curve (L) is tangent to the iso-vote curve. This constellation is reached in point V^{**} in Figure 10.6. In this long-run vote maximum V^{**}, a vote share of 53 per cent is attained. It is,

FIG. 10.6. *Vote maximum with constant policy (steady-state equilibrium)*

however, quite possible that a constant economic policy does not yield a sufficient vote share for survival. In this case a vote-maximising government can attempt to reach re-election by a variation in the rates of unemployment and inflation over the course of the election period.

Stable political business cycles

The following policy is optimal for a vote-maximising government willing to steer the economy in the short run.

After the election, unemployment is increased in order to depress inflationary expectations. This policy has a negative effect only for a short period. It is, at the same time, an 'investment', as it shifts the short-run Phillips Curve towards the origin for the following years. The conflict between unemployment and inflation is therefore mitigated towards the election date. In the following two years unemployment is gradually reduced. In the election year, the government attempts to reach the lowest unemployment rate and, thereby, the highest rate of inflation.

This vote-maximising political business cycle, which is repeated in each election period (provided there are no exogenous influences), is shown in Figure 10.7. The development of the vote-maximising politico-economic cycle sketched takes place if voters evaluate the government according to economic conditions in the

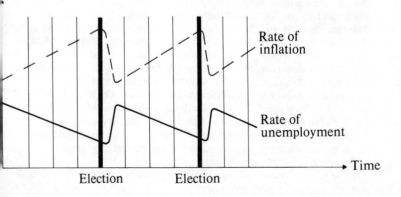

FIG. 10.7. *Vote-maximising election cycle*

election year. It may, however, also appear if the preceding years of an election period are part of the evaluation with a constant or decreasing weight.

ELECTION CYCLES: CAUSES AND EMPIRICAL OBSERVATIONS

Conditions for their appearance

The regular swings of the politico-economic system discussed in the previous section may be called *election cycles* because they are due to the government's re-election requirement and their length equals exactly one election period. Election cycles may be due to three causes.

(1) *Restricted time-horizon of the voters.* Voters evaluate the government's performance according to economic conditions of the past legislative period and do not account for the economic repercussions brought about by government policy undertaken *before* the election but arising only in the subsequent election period. The voters can deter the government from undertaking such a policy by withdrawing their votes when the government intends to undertake the corresponding economic actions. To be successful, voters must make a completely rational and strategic vote decision and, moreover, must possess the same level of information as the government. Such conditions are unlikely to be met in reality.

(2) *Restricted time-horizon of the government.* The election cycle was derived for a government intending to maximise its share of the votes at the next election. The period thereafter is completely left out of account. The time-horizon should not, however, be taken as fixed; it essentially depends on the *re-election chances*. A government confident of its re-election has no reason to value the next legislative period less highly than the present one (except for the usual discounting of the future). A government that expects to win all forthcoming elections has no reason to maximise votes and to introduce an election cycle. On the other hand, a government that fears losing the forthcoming election does not expect to be in existence in the next election period and, accordingly, its time-horizon will end at this election date. The assumption of a time-horizon of only one election period, made in the model discussed above, is appropriate for that extreme case only.

(3) *Use of the dynamic properties of the economic system.* In the model discussed above it is advantageous to the government to make an *investment* at the beginning of an election period by pursuing a restrictive policy (i.e. increasing unemployment) in order to dampen voters'

inflationary expectations and to reach a more favourable trade-off between unemployment and inflation towards the end of the election period. A government may also use *time-lags* inherent in the economic system for election purposes. Price increases or increases in the rate of inflation as a rule take place *after* an upswing in production and *after* a reduction in the rate of unemployment. If the government is not sure of being re-elected (and that is the case in a democracy), it does not place great value on the price increases that will occur in the ensuing election period because they may possibly burden the government formed by the (present) opposition party (or parties). In this case it may be advantageous to the government to secure rapid income growth and high employment by means of an expansionary policy. If, nevertheless, the election is lost, the induced high inflation will affect the (present) opposition; this increases the chance of the present government's returning to power soon.

Empirical observations

Cycles in unemployment and inflation

Does there exist in reality an *election cycle* like that schematically pictured in Figure 10.7? The way in which the rate of unemployment has developed in the United Kingdom over the six election periods from 1952 to 1974 is shown in Figure 10.8. The

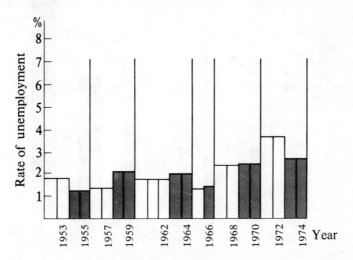

Fig. 10.8. *Rates of unemployment over the six election periods 1952–74 (United Kingdom)*

election periods (which for simplicity are taken to cover complete years) are divided into two parts; the values for the two pre-election years (with the exception of the term 1965–66) are shaded.

According to the vote-maximising election cycle presented in the last section, the rate of unemployment should be lower in the second half than in the first half of the election period. In the United Kingdom this holds only for the two election periods of 1952–55 and 1971–74. In the election periods of 1956–59 and 1960–64 the rate of unemployment was clearly higher in the second part compared with the first part of the term.

Figure 10.9 shows the corresponding development of the *rate of inflation*. According to the vote-maximising model discussed above, the inflation rate should be higher in the second half of the election term than in the first half. This is true for the last two election terms of 1967–70 and 1971–74. During the other election periods the

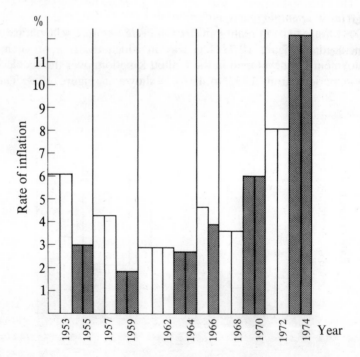

FIG. 10.9. *Rates of inflation over the six election periods 1952–74 (United Kingdom)*

inflation rate was lower in the years before than after an election. It should be noted that there is a trend increase in the rate of inflation since the beginning of the 1960s. Looking at the development of these two macroeconomic variables, there is, at least for the United Kingdom, little evidence for the particular vote-maximising election cycle theoretically derived.

Figures 10.10 and 10.11 show the development of the rate of unemployment and the rate of inflation in the United States over the six presidential election periods from 1953 to 1976. The two pre-election years of the regular four-year presidential term are again shaded. The rate of unemployment was lower in the second half of the term under the administrations of Presidents Kennedy and Johnson, 1961–64 and 1965–68. Under the Nixon and Ford administrations (1969–72 and 1973–76) unemployment was much higher in the second part of the term.

The rate of inflation is *clearly* higher in the second than in the first half in only one election period (1965–68). In three election periods (1957–60, 1969–72 and 1973–76), inflation strongly decreased in the second half.

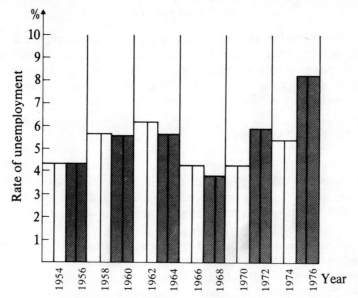

FIG. 10.10. *Rates of unemployment over six presidential election periods 1953–76 (United States)*

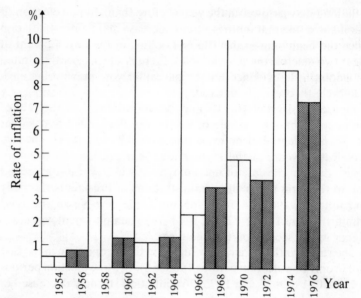

FIG. 10.11. *Rates of inflation over six presidential election terms 1953–76 (United States)*

The conclusion drawn for the United Kingdom is supported by the figures shown for the United States. There is no compelling evidence for a vote-maximising election cycle theoretically derived above as manifested in the development of two important macro-economic variables, unemployment and inflation.

Cycles in income growth
In connection with the dynamic properties of the economic system as a cause for political business cycles, it was suggested that an expansionary policy during the pre-election years benefits a government seeking re-election. It is thus expected that the *rate of growth of income* is larger in the years preceding an election than in the years directly following one.

An empirical analysis of twenty-seven democracies over the period from 1960–71 shows that in twenty-one of these countries (among them the UK, the US, Canada and Australia) the growth rate of real disposable income was higher in election years than in non-election years. In only three countries is the evidence against the existence of an election cycle thus defined, and in three further countries there is no difference between election and non-election years with respect to income growth. If the election period is again divided into pre-election and post-election years as in the preceding figures, there is no very convincing evidence for a political cycle in terms of income growth in the United Kingdom. This is shown in Figure 10.12.

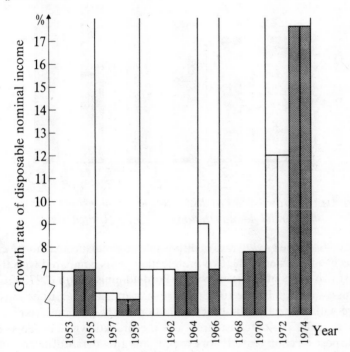

FIG. 10.12. *Growth rates of disposable nominal income over the six election periods 1952–74 (United Kingdom)*

The percentage rate of increase in disposable nominal income was *clearly* higher before the elections (compared with thereafter) only in the last two election periods (1967–70 and 1971–74). In the 1966 election the growth rate was considerably lower than in 1965, but it should be noted that the election was early in 1966 (31 March). In the other election periods there is no clear difference between pre- and post-election years.

In the United States a political business cycle is clearly visible in the first three election periods considered (1953–56, 1957–60, and

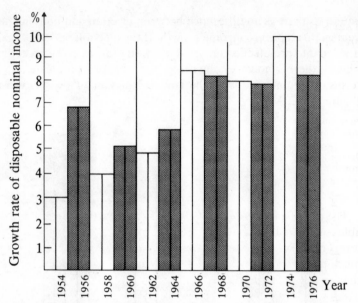

FIG. 10.13. *Growth rates of disposable nominal income over the six presidential administrations 1953–76 (United States)*

1961–64). The growth rate of disposable nominal income, however, was clearly lower in the two pre-election years compared with the first two years of the joint Nixon–Ford administration (1973–76). This is shown in Figure 10.13. The results are, however, quite sensitive with respect to the exact definition of the economic variable chosen, the period considered and the breakdown between pre- and post-election years. If, for example, the growth rate of disposable *real* (instead of nominal) income in the presidential election year is compared with its value in three non-election years over a forty-year period, an election cycle becomes more apparent. This is shown in Table 10.1. The growth rate of income increased in *all* presidential election years (up to 1973). In the years with no presidential elections income growth increased in twenty-four years only (i.e. in 77 per cent of the years), and decreased in seven years.

If both presidential *and* congressional elections are considered, the kind of political business cycle discussed becomes even more marked: in fourteen out of eighteen years an increase in the growth rate of disposable real income and a subsequent decrease in the following (non-election) year may be observed.

TABLE 10.1. *The growth rate of disposable real income in US presidential election years compared with other years, 1933–73*

	Year with presidential election	Years without presidential election
Increasing growth rate	10	24
Decreasing growth rate	0	7

The clearest evidence of an election cycle, in the aggregate variable considered, exists for Israel. With the exception of one election term (1962–65) the growth rate in *per capita* consumption was very much higher in the two years preceding an election to the Knesset than in the years thereafter. This is shown in Figure 10.14.

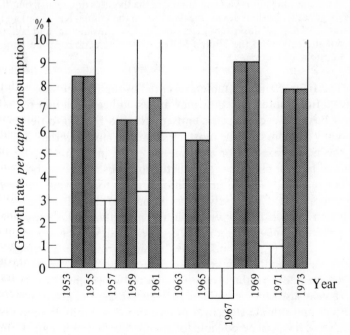

FIG. 10.14. *Growth rates of* per capita *consumption over six election periods 1952–73 (Israel)*

THEORY AND EMPIRICAL EVIDENCE

The empirical evidence of the political business cycle offered in the last section creates a mixed impression. Though there were some cases in which such a cycle could be detected (especially with respect to income and consumption growth), it was, on the whole, not possible to identify a clear and regular election cycle.

There may be several reasons why such cycles could not be found in the aggregate data considered, the three most important ones of which are as follows.

(1) National economies may depend on each other to such an extent, through international trade, capital movements and price changes (such as the recent sudden increase in oil and other resource prices), that a possibly existing political cycle becomes invisible.
(2) 'Pure' economic (national) business cycles of the traditional type may be strong enough to swamp election cycles.
(3) In many countries there is not simply one general election occurring at regular time intervals (as assumed in the theories discussed), but there are general elections at varying dates (as in the United Kingdom) and/or various *kinds* of important elections (such as presidential and congressional elections in the United States, or state elections in the Federal Republic of Germany).

The figures and the table presented in the last section can only give a first impression: they may at best indicate whether the political business cycle is sufficiently marked to be said to determine directly the course of the most important economic variables. Even if this is the case (as for example for Israel in Figure 10.14), one should bear in mind that the fluctuations observed *may* be due to other reasons, such as the traditional four- to five-year economic business cycle. Conversely, if (as in many of the other figures) no election cycle is clearly visible in the macro-variables considered, this does not mean that no such cycle exists: it may be swamped by other effects (e.g. by influences coming from the international sphere). A careful empirical study requires an *isolation* of the election cycle: all influences not connected with it must be excluded.

If such disturbing exogenous effects are kept constant with the help of appropriate statistical procedures (e.g. multiple regression analysis), it would be possible to find out whether or not an election cycle exists. In order to be able to undertake such an isolation, it is necessary to have a clear conception of the underlying model of the political business cycle. On the basis of theoretical deliberations, the exact properties of the election cycle to be tested must be identified. This allows us to keep constant those factors in the empirical analysis that are not considered relevant from the theoretical point of view. The empirical test is not applied to *some* kind of political cycle, but to a clear theoretical notion of it.

A carefully formulated theoretical model has to specify exactly in what way the government creates a political business cycle. Thus government behaviour can be related more closely to fluctuations in the economy. This reduces the danger that theoretical expectations and empirical observations are taken to correspond to each other, when in fact they do not.

The following chapter shows how the mutual interdependence of economy and polity may be empirically tested with a politico-economic model that meets the requirements discussed.

LITERATURE

A survey of politico-economic models is given in
>Bruno S. Frey and Friedrich Schneider, 'On the Modelling of Politico-Economic Interdependence'. *European Journal of Political Research*, 3 (1975).

The discussed model of a vote-maximising government confronted with the inflation–unemployment trade-off is due to
>William D. Nordhaus, 'The Political Business Cycle'. *Review of Economic Studies*, 42 (1975).

Nordhaus's conclusion that democratic governments are extremely myopic is disputed by
>Bruno S. Frey and Hans-Juergen Ramser, 'The Political Business Cycle: Comment'. *Review of Economic Studies*, 43 (1976).

The following model is quite similar to the one by Nordhaus but is also concerned with voters' rational behaviour and with the possibility of preventing election cycles by strategic voting:
>Duncan MacRae, 'A Political Model of the Business Cycle'. *Journal of Political Economy*, 85 (1977).

An extended discussion of the elements and various types of formal politico-economic models is given in
>Bruno S. Frey, 'Politico-Economic Models and Cycles'. *Journal of Public Economics*, 8 (1978).

The figures in the text are based on data collected from *Main Economic Indicators* of OECD, Paris (various years), and from the *Annual Abstract of*

Statistics, HMSO, London (various years). The analysis of the twenty-seven democracies in Table 10.1 are due to

Edward R. Tufte, 'The Political Manipulation of the Economy: Influence of the Electoral Cycle on Macroeconomic Performance and Policy'. *American Political Science Review*, (forthcoming).

The figure on the election cycle in Israel is taken from

Yoram Ben-Porath, 'The Years of Plenty and the Years of Famine: A Political Business Cycle?' *Kyklos*, 28 (1975).

11. The Overall Interaction between Economy and Polity Analysed Quantitatively

TOTAL POLITICO-ECONOMIC MODELS

Total politico-economic models analyse the overall inter-dependence of economy and polity. Restrictions on modelling are required here, too: only very few of the most important politico-economic decision-makers are considered. Government activity is again at the centre of attention; it constitutes the decisive link between economic and political forces.

In the model developed here and empirically tested with data for the United Kingdom and the United States, the government is assumed to *maximise its own utility subject to a re-election constraint*. Besides this political restriction, the government must also take into account economic and administrative constraints. This behavioural model has been discussed theoretically in Chapter 7.

Government action is determined mainly by economic con-ditions, as voters hold the government responsible for an unfavour-able state of economy. During the election term public opinion polls serve the government as indicators of the likely future election outcome. This relationship between economic variables and gov-ernment popularity is captured by the *popularity function*. If, owing to a low popularity index, re-election is in danger, the government uses policy instruments to improve economic conditions. It will consider both the time available until the next election takes place and the time period until economic policy actions have an effect. If public opinion polls point to a comfortable re-election, the gov-ernment can afford economic actions that correspond to its ideolog-ical position even if they do *not* necessarily bring votes.

Such government behaviour is described by the *policy function*. The total interdependence between the economy and polity described is illustrated in Figure 11.1. The lower loop going from the economy to government indicates the *popularity function*. The upper loop leading from government via the civil service to the economy shows the *policy function*. In this simple model government popularity is determined by the economic variables of unemployment, inflation and growth of income. The use of economic policy instruments consisting of (exhaustive) public expenditures for goods and services and transfers depends on ideology and re-election expectation, as well as on the state of the budget. There is also an independent influence of the civil service.

The politico-economic model sketched has been analytically formulated in various versions and its properties have been tested with the help of computer simulations. The use of analytical versions is restricted by the limited possibility of manipulation, while simulations have a limited usefulness because every conceivable time-path may be traced by an appropriate choice of parameter values. For these reasons the models are empirically tested. Such a formal estimation of politico-economic models may – in analogy with econometrics – be called *politometrics*.

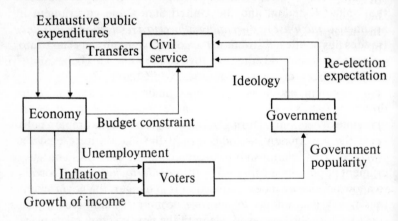

FIG. 11.1. *The total politico-economic model used*

GOVERNMENT POPULARITY

Survey research institutes regularly collect data on government popularity. In the United Kingdom, Gallup and National Opinion

Polls ask an almost identical question in their voting intention surveys; 'If there were a General Election tomorrow, which party would you support?' As already indicated, current economic conditions influence the answer to this question. If economic conditions are good, a larger share of the people asked will tend to support the party in government; if economic conditions are unfavourable, people will tend to support the opposition. It has been found that the population does not take into account (or only very little) whether government or influences beyond the government's control are responsible for the economic situation existing; neither is it considered how far the state of the economy is due to the previous government's policy, or if the party now in opposition would be capable of pursuing a better economic policy. Voters disregard these factors when answering the survey questions because it would require a fair amount of effort to consider them all, which is not thought worthwhile to an individual.

Government popularity is determined not only by economic variables but also by the amount of time that has passed since the last election. It is a common observation in many countries that the government becomes more unpopular the longer it has been in office, which may be called popularity depreciation. In the empirical estimates of the popularity function presented in the following, these influences are captured by dummy variables.

The general estimation equation is

Popularity (t) = const. + a_1 [unemployment, $U(t)$] + a_2 [inflation, $I(t)$] + a_3 [growth of income, $G(t)$] + a_4[popularity depreciation, $DEP(t)$] + $\varepsilon(t)$.

Government popularity depends negatively on the current rate of unemployment U and on the rate of inflation I, and positively on the rate of growth of real disposable income G. The empirical estimates of the parameters are thus expected to be $a_1 < 0$, $a_2 < 0$, and $a_3 > 0$. The variable popularity depreciation DEP is captured by a dummy variable which increases over time as measured from the previous election; because government popularity is expected to wane over the course of the election period, the corresponding parameter is expected to be negative $(a_4 < 0)$.

The estimation equation presented above must be further adjusted if it is applied to particular countries in order to take account of historical and institutional differences.

Estimates for the United Kingdom

The British political system is composed of two major parties, Conservative and Labour. The party having the larger number of MPs elected on a constituency basis forms the government; i.e., the *lead* (over the main opposition party) is decisive. For this reason lead, and not popularity, is taken to be the dependent variable to be explained.

A special feature of the British system also is the variable election date (within five years from the last one). It may be assumed that the prime minister does not call an election before (about) four years have passed if he has a safe parliamentary base (an overall majority of, say, ten or more seats).

Empirical observation suggests that in the United Kingdom the government's lead not only falls over the course of an election period (this is captured by the depreciation variable), but that there is also a swing of voter support *back* to the government when a general election is expected to be announced. This special effect is accounted for by a variable quantity counting the number of quarters to the nearest election, *NE*. This variable seeks to capture the fall and revival of the government lead throughout the election term.

The lead function is estimated (by ordinary least squares regression) with quarterly data for 1959: IV to 1974: IV, thus covering the governments of Macmillan, Douglas-Home (October 1963–October 1964), Wilson (October 1964–June 1970), Heath (June 1970–March 1974), and again Wilson (March 1974 to the end of the estimation period). The estimate is:

$$LEAD(t) = 10.24 - 6.0\,U(t) - 0.6\,I(t) + 0.8\,G(t) - 0.6\,DEP(t)$$
$$ (-3.9)\quad (-2.7)\quad (+2.9)\quad (-4.5)$$

$$-0.7\,NE(t);$$
$$(-2.4)$$

$$R^2 = 0.7, DW = 1.7$$

The figures in parentheses below the parameter estimates are the
t-values. A value of more than (about) ± 2 indicates that the corresponding parameter estimate is statistically significantly different
from 0 with a degree of confidence of 95 per cent. As may be seen,
all the parameter estimates meet this test. Moreover, they all have
the theoretically expected sign: an increase in the rate of unemployment by one percentage point decreases government lead by six
percentage points. The influence of inflation is less strong; if it
increases by one per cent, government lead falls by only 0.6 per
cent. A rise of the real growth rate of disposable income increases
the government's popularity lead by 0.8 per cent. The so-called
'pure election cycle' is clearly visible: the government lead continually depreciates over the term, but there also is a revival before
an election (-0.6 and -0.7, respectively). The equation as a whole
explains (in the statistical sense) about 70 per cent of the variance
($\bar{R}^2 = 0.7$); and the Durbin–Watson test statistic indicates absence
of serial correlation ($DW = 1.7$); i.e. there is reason to assume that
the parameter estimates are unbiased.

Estimates for the United States

In the United States the executive is strongly shaped by the personality of the president. For this reason the president's popularity
is taken as the dependent variable, and a particular popularity *level*
is introduced for each president. It is also taken into account that
presidents may have different rates of depreciation of their popularity over the election term. President Nixon suffered such an
extraordinary and dramatic loss of confidence in his second
(unfinished) term that a special Watergate dummy variable (WAT)
is introduced which takes the value 1,3,5,5,5 from the second
quarter of 1973 to the second quarter of 1974. The respective
parameter estimate is expected to be negative. The influence of
inflation is lagged by one quarter (this is a minor change).

The estimates with quarterly data extend over the period from
1953: I to 1975: II and thus cover two (Republican) Eisenhower
administrations (1953:I–1960:IV), the (Democratic) administrations of Kennedy (1961:I–1963:IV) and Johnson (1964:
I–1968:IV), and the (Republican) administrations of Nixon
(1969:I–1974:II) and Ford (1974:III–1975:II). The popularity
function estimated is:

$$POP(t) = - 4.0 \ U(t) - 1.0 \ I(t-1) + 0.5 \ G(t) - 0.1 \ DEP_E$$
$$ (-5.2) \qquad (-2.0) \qquad\quad (1.7) \qquad (-0.4)$$

$$-1.2 \ DEP_{KJ} - 0.3 \ DEP_N - 4.7 \ WAT + 79.0 \ E_I +$$
$$(-4.6) \qquad\quad (-1.0) \qquad\quad (-4.0) \qquad\quad (11.3)$$

$$+ \ 64.8 \ E_2 + 76.0 \ K + 68.4 \ J + 62.6 \ N + 76.0 \ F.$$
$$(15.8) \qquad (19.5) \qquad (17.1) \qquad (10.5) \qquad (7.1)$$

$$\bar{R}^2 = 0.9, \ DW = 2.0$$

In this estimate not all parameters are statistically different from 0, in particular the rate of growth of real income G. By more refined statistical manipulations it may be shown that this economic variable *does* have a significant effect on presidential popularity. (The seemingly insignificant result is due to multicollinearity between the economic variables.) The signs of the coefficients correspond (with two exceptions) to theoretical expectations. An increase in the rate of unemployment by one percentage point decreases presidential popularity by about four percentage points. If the rate of inflation increases by one per cent, popularity also drops by one per cent, and an increase in the growth rate of real income by one per cent lifts the president's popularity on the average by 0.5 per cent.

Kennedy and Johnson's joint popularity depreciated (DEP_{KJ}) strongly over their term of office, which may partly be due to the unpopular war in Vietnam. The Watergate scandal (WAT) had an even stronger effect on Nixon's popularity. Eisenhower's (E) and Nixon's $(N$, first term only) popularity decrease is not statistically significant. The highest personal popularity *level* was enjoyed by President Eisenhower in his first term (E_1) with a (theoretical) share of approval of 79 per cent, and by Presidents Kennedy (K) and Ford (F) with 76 per cent. followed by Johnson (J) with 68.4 per cent. At the bottom according to this ranking are Eisenhower in his second term (E_2) with 64.8 per cent, and finally Nixon (N) with 62.6 per cent.

The equation as a whole is able statistically to explain over 90 per cent of the variance $(\bar{R}^2 = 0.9)$, and the parameter estimates may be taken to be unbiased $(DW = 2.0)$.

The politometric estimates presented suggest that, if a government (at least in these two countries) wants to increase its popularity and re-election chances, it does well to pursue an *expansionary* policy, which lowers unemployment and increases economic growth. Only a very rapid and immediate rise of the rate of inflation (which seems quite unlikely) would prevent an increase in the government's popularity or lead.

GOVERNMENT POLICY

The party in power considers as its main goal putting its ideological views into reality. It must, however, ensure that it remains in office, because in opposition it has no possibility of realising its ideology. The government is also forced to take into account the state of the budget; i.e., it may not extend public expenditures too far relative to tax income. In some countries there are other important economic restrictions, in particular the balance of payments. The government is thus assumed to maximise its own utility (consisting of its ideological views) subject to the re-election constraint and economic constraints (budget and balance of payments constraints).

To solve this intertemporal maximisation problem formally would be far beyond the capacity of a government; the informational aspects alone are extremely difficult to cope with. Government politicians, therefore, use a simplified method to solve the problem intuitively. They (rightly) take the political surveys as a good (and currently the only available) indicator for future election outcome; in particular, they assume that a certain popularity share (POP^*) – say 58 per cent of the people asked – makes re-election quite certain. If current surveys indicate that popularity is higher, i.e. if there exists a *popularity surplus* ($POP \geqslant POP^*$), the government can pursue an ideological policy. It is expected that a left-wing party tends to increase and a right-wing party to decrease public expenditures. If, however, the surveys point to a *popularity deficit* ($POP < POP^*$), the government must make an effort to pursue a policy agreeable to the voters. As mentioned above this is achieved by an expansionary policy, i.e. by increasing public expenditures. The nearer the forthcoming elections are, the more difficult becomes the government's position and the more strongly must the economic policy instruments be used in order to bring about an increase in its popularity.

As shown in Figure 11.1, the civil service also has an influence on the use of economic policy instruments. It has an interest in continually expanding the budget and in resisting structural changes in expenditures. This influence as well as legal restrictions may be captured by introducing the previous expenditure level among the explanatory variables.

Public expenditures are thus determined by four factors:

(1) government ideology in the case of a popularity surplus;
(2) re-election effort in the case of a popularity deficit;
(3) economic constraints imposed by the budget and balance of payments constraints;
(4) administrative (bureaucratic) and legal constraints.

Estimates for the United Kingdom

Table 11.1 shows the *politometric estimates* for consumption and transfer expenditures (to the personal sector) in the United Kingdom. The period extends from 1962: II to 1974: IV, i.e. covers the governments of Macmillan (only the last year and a half, to October 1963), Douglas-Home, Wilson, Heath, and again Wilson. The complete model, the exact definition of the variables and the data used are explained in the works quoted at the end of this chapter. The budget constraint is not included as a determinant because tax income is endogenously explained (not shown here). Government popularity is again substituted by government *lead*. Additional determinants introduced are cost factors (lagged wage rate and price level).

All the parameters (with two exceptions) are statistically significantly different from zero, as indicated by the t-values below the coefficients in Table 11.1. All the parameters have the expected sign. If a popularity surplus allows it, right-wing (Conservative) governments tend to spend less ($\beta_C < 0$) and left-wing (Labour) governments tend to spend more ($\beta_L > 0$). In case of a popularity deficit, all governments embark on an expansionary policy by increasing expenditures ($\beta_2 > 0$), and they do that more strongly the nearer the expected elections are ($\beta_3 < 0$). The more favourable the balance of payments, the more is spent ($\beta_4 > 0$). The administrative and legal constraints represented by the lagged expenditures have a positive influence ($\beta_5 > 0$). An increase in wages and prices tends to blow up public expenditures ($\beta_6 > 0$, $\beta_7 > 0$).

The equation as a whole explains a very high share of the variance

TABLE 11.1. *Policy function for the United Kingdom, 1962:II–1974:IV*

Policy instrument	Ideological determinants			Re-election effort			Constraints			$\bar{R}^2$	DW
	Constant β_0	Conservatives β_C	Labour β_L	Lead deficit β_2	Expected time to election β_3	Balance of payments β_4	Administrative & legal β_5	Cost Factors Wages β_6	Prices β_7		
Consumption	-0.63	-0.003 (-1.4)	0.008 (2.2)	0.007 (2.1)	-0.004 (-2.2)	0.0002 (3.4)	0.38 (2.1)	0.013 (2.8)	0.039 (2.4)	0.99	1.73
Transfers	-0.46	-0.004 (-2.1)	0.005 (2.3)	0.005 (2.4)	-0.005 (-2.0)	0.0001 (2.5)	0.10 (2.8)	0.008 (1.4)	0.014 (3.5)	0.99	1.70

($\bar{R}^2 = 0.99$), and the parameter estimates do not seem to be biased (Durbin–Watson coefficient around 1.7).

Estimates for the United States

Table 11.2 presents the politometric estimates of public expenditures for the United States. The variables explained are civilian government expenditures for goods and services and transfers to households. They cover the same period as the popularity function estimated above. The ideological bias in times of popularity surplus refers to individual presidents, because in the United States party affiliation of the government leader is of much less importance than it is, for example, in the United Kingdom. The budget constraint is taken into account by including tax receipts among the explanatory variables. The higher taxes are, the higher expenditures may be without running into an (additional) budget deficit. The balance of payments constraint is not included, owing to its unimportance for the United States. Details of the estimate can again be found in the literature quoted at the end of this chapter.

All parameters referring to re-election effort and constraints (with one exception) are statistically significant. According to these estimates, American presidents do not seem to have an ideology that would fit the simple spectrum assumed. Only Nixon has significantly reduced both types of expenditures (*ceteris paribus*) when he enjoyed a popularity surplus ($\gamma_N < 0$). This corresponds to a priori expectations, as Nixon's ideology can certainly be considered 'right-wing'; though a 'left-wing' politician, Johnson, significantly reduced civilian expenditures ($\gamma_3 > 0$), which may be due to the high requirements for military purposes going with the Vietnam War.

All statistically significant parameters are in accordance with theoretical expectations. The larger the size of the popularity deficit, the more expansionary is economic policy ($\gamma_1 > 0$). The re-election effort is increased the less time there is until the next election takes place ($\gamma_2 < 0$). The higher tax receipts, the higher are public expenditures ($\gamma_J > 0$). As in the United Kingdom, there is a positive influence of administrative (bureaucratic) and legal constraints (represented by past expenditures) on current outlays ($\gamma_4 > 0$).

The policy equation explains a high share of the variance ($\bar{R}^2 = 0.99$), and the parameter estimates seem to be unbiased.

TABLE 11.2. *Policy function for the United States, 1953:II–1975:II*

Policy instrument	const. γ_0	Ideological determinants				Re-election efforts		Constraints		$\bar{R}^2$	DW
		Eisenhower γ_E	Kennedy γ_K	Johnson γ_J	Nixon γ_N	Popularity deficit γ_1	Time to election γ_2	Budget (tax receipts) γ_3	Administrative & legal γ_4		
Civilian expenditure	-0.45	-0.0003 (-0.8)	0.0001 (1.3)	-0.0003 (-2.1)	-0.0005 (-2.0)	0.0002 (2.5)	-0.37 (3.4)	0.08 (5.4)	0.64 (9.2)	0.99	1.6
Transfers	-2.21	0.001 (0.8)	-0.0007 (-0.5)	-0.002 (-0.6)	-0.0004 (-2.4)	0.002 (2.6)	-0.03 (-0.5)	0.11 (2.4)	1.03 (11.7)	0.99	1.5

EVIDENCE OF A POLITICAL BUSINESS CYCLE

As will be remembered from the last chapter, there was little and
unclear evidence about the existence of a political business cycle
when aggregate time-series data are looked at graphically. The
estimation results presented here for both countries suggest, however, that governments are well aware of the effect of economic
policy measures upon their popularity, and that they do indeed use
economic policy instruments in order to secure their re-election.
The multiple regression technique employed allows us to separate
this activity from other influences, such as the need to balance the
budget or autonomous bureaucratic activity. The approach also
allows us to isolate clearly those time periods in which the government is really actively concerned with re-election. The results of
the empirical estimates show that – all other things being equal –
British and American governments pursue an expansionary policy
before elections, when they are unsure about their re-election. In
this case they *actively* produce an election cycle. The partial regression coefficients showing the influence of the time remaining until
the election have a negative and (with one exception) statistically
significant negative sign (see the parameters β_3 in Table 11.1 and γ_2
in Table 11.2). The less time there is until election, the higher
(*ceteris paribus*) are public expenditures for goods and services and
for transfers to private households.

USE OF TOTAL POLITICO-ECONOMIC MODELS AND FURTHER
DEVELOPMENTS

The politico-economic approach developed may be useful for two
different purposes. In order to *explain* and to *forecast* the interaction between the economy and polity, the closed model with both
loops of interdependence must be used. For purposes of economic
policy, the main interest lies in the effects of economic policy
measures upon popularity and therefore on the survival chance of
the government. Advisors and government politicians are given
information that may be of central importance for the policies to be
undertaken.

The politico-econometric models sketched consider only few

actors. Among the important decision-makers, the central bank, interest groups, parliament and its commissions, federal units as well as governments of other nations are missing. The model also has some weaknesses with respect to its structure. The relationship between government popularity and election success, for example, is not yet fully clarified; no theory of coalition formation among parties is included; etc. The approach furthermore is strongly concentrated on the discontinuity introduced by elections; it is necessary to include additional, election-independent institutional determinants of politico-economic processes. Besides this, there is an additional feedback mechanism by which the government can influence voters' evaluation of the state of the economy. This possibility is also used by opposition parties and interest groups.

The empirically tested models of macro-relationships between economy and polity differ in various respects from the purely neoclassical approaches forming the basis of public choice. Some of the characteristics stressed by the unorthodox political economists (see Chapter 5) are taken into account in the models. The differences are most obvious when the politico-economic models are compared with the theory of party competition (see Chapter 7):

(1) politics is not seen as the fight for votes among parties in analogy to the market; rather, the *dominating role of government*, with a decision space and an ideology of its own, is stressed;
(2) there is no analysis of equilibrium; what matters are the *evolutionary processes* that try to capture the temporal sequence;
(3) *economic relationships* are explicitly introduced and the instruments available to government are specified.

The combination of elements of public choice and of the political economy of the Unorthodox may help to make sure that the total politico-economic models continue to be concerned with reality (instead of with abstract modelling for its own sake), and that the approach maintains its flexibility. Like every other branch of research, it runs the danger of becoming esoteric and sterile. In each case it must be carefully considered whether or not extensions of the models yield relevant new knowledge.

LITERATURE

The present chapter is based on research undertaken by the author together with his collaborator Friedrich Schneider.

An empirical model for the United Kingdom similar to that presented here is more fully discussed in

> Bruno S. Frey and Friedrich Schneider, 'A Politico-Economic Model of the United Kingdom'. *Economic Journal*, 88 (1978).

A general quantitative survey of the British political system is given in

> David Butler and Anne Sloman, *British Political Facts 1900–1975*. Macmillan, London, 1975.

The politico-economic model of the United States discussed is based on

> Bruno S. Frey and Friedrich Schneider, 'An Empirical Study of Politico-Economic Interaction in the U.S.' *Review of Economics and Statistics*, 60 (1978).

A similar model has been developed for the Federal Republic of Germany with yearly data by

> Bruno S. Frey and Friedrich Schneider, 'An Econometric Model with an Endogenous Government Sector'. *Public Choice*, 33 (1978).

In this model the (*ex post*) forecasts undertaken with the politico-economic model are compared with those of a 'pure' econometric model. It turns out that the politico-economic model performs much better.

Part V

WHAT CAN BE LEARNT FROM POLITICAL ECONOMY?

The concluding part of this book takes up some of the theories developed and relates them to each other. The important interdependencies between economy and polity – which are disregarded in traditional economic theory – are studied in the context of a modern society. For this purpose public choice based on neoclassical economics and the political economy of the Unorthodox are combined to form a new political economy. The discussion of evolutionary processes in the area of public goods and the infrastructure and the empirical analysis of aggregate politico-economic models are two applications of the latter.

The new political economy may be further developed in various directions. The interdependency between economy and polity must be better understood, and besides positive theory there must be a *normative* theory analysing the possibilities for change on the basis of a closed politico-economic system. The methods applied in this book constitute *one* way of interdisciplinary research designed to relate economy and polity to each other; it may be expanded into psychological, sociological and ethnological areas.

12. The New Political Economy

The close interdependence of economy and polity cannot be disputed, but it is scarcely considered in traditional economics. The increasing importance of government activity and of economic relationships outside the market makes it more and more impossible for economics, committed to the price system and disregarding institutions, to contribute to the understanding of modern society. The behaviour of public and private decision-makers in the political area needs to be explained.

The mutual relationship between economy and polity can be analysed in various ways. The goal and the methodological approach constitute the major characteristics of each type of analysis. There are many variants of modern political economy. The political economy of the Unorthodox should be paid particular attention to because it is a fruitful alternative to orthodox economics. The Unorthodox make an effort to analyse the pressing problems of today's society and they add to the discussion new standpoints, fresh ideas and original models of solution.

Great attention must also be paid to *public choice*, which analyses political processes with the style of thinking and the instruments of modern neoclassical economic theory, and which thereby endeavours to integrate economy and polity. By this approach the basic problem of every political decision, the aggregation of individual preferences to a social decision, can be analysed precisely. Within public choice, institutions such as government, political parties, interest groups and the civil service are studied. No description is intended, but rather a causal explanation is made of the behaviour of such institutions, with the help of simple hypotheses such as vote and utility maximisation.

The two variants of political economy at the centre of the present examination have strengths and weaknesses. The strength of public choice lies in the application of a simple method to both the economy *and* the polity in such a way that it is possible to connect the two areas closely while maintaining theoretical rigour. The strength of the political economy of the Unorthodox lies in its innovation concerning assumptions and results, the study of important problems, and the lack of respect with which problems that are traditionally considered important are treated. The weakness of public choice lies in its narrowness and often irrelevance of assumption, the mere play with models, the overstress of mathematics in comparison with the often weak content of the results. The weakness of the political economy of the Unorthodox lies in the incoherence and sometimes the inconsistency of arguments, and in its negligence to carefully state the assumptions and precisely derive the results.

This discussion makes clear that the two approaches may complement each other. The weakness of one variant to a large extent is the strength of the other. It is, therefore, useful to combine them in a new political economy, which exploits the strength of each variant. A good possibility is offered by the study of *evolutionary development processes* such as may arise owing to the demand for and supply of infrastructure and public goods. This process develops in a cyclical pattern. The revelation of demand as well as the coming about of supply are the result of an interaction of economy and polity prohibiting uniform and immediate adaptation.

It is often argued that political economy may be on the right track, but that its conclusions may not be *statistically* tested and that, therefore, they are of little use.

Indeed, it is true that most variants of political economy, including the two mentioned above, pay little attention to empirical research. The representatives of the political economy of the Unorthodox do not use systematic statistical tests in order to support their arguments; at best they collect some figures and present them in tables. The theories presented on the overall social relationships are not open to strict statistical analysis because frequently they are too general to be verified. In the axiomatically formulated public choice theory – in particular in the case of the theorems on preference aggregation – it is at best possible to test the realism of the basic assumptions made. Often these assumptions have the character of normative propositions – as for example the condition of the independence of irrelevant alternatives – the empirical content of which is irrelevant. It is surprising that the behavioural theories of politico-economic decision-makers have been empirically analysed so little, despite the fact that one of the main claims of this branch of public choice lies in the possibility of comparing the theories with reality. Only the median voter model has been tested frequently and successfully, but it should be remembered that it is appropriate only for the case of a democracy in which *all* voters regularly meet in an assembly.

The combination of the two variants in a new political economy allows us quantitatively to study overall relationships between economy and polity. The politico-economic models with time-series data for the post-war period show that voters evaluate a government's performance mainly according to the state of the economy. A decrease in the rate of inflation and in the rate of unemployment, and a rise in the rate of growth of income, increases the government's popularity and thereby its chance of staying in power. The government uses its instruments of economic policy not – as is often suggested – to further 'social welfare', but rather to increase its re-election chances. If, on the other hand, the government is confident of re-election, it endeavours to make its ideological ideas become true. Governments orientated towards the right have the tendency to decrease public expenditures; governments of the left tend to increase them. Governments concerned about their re-election create *political business cycles* by increasing public outlays before the election and thus bringing about a more rapid expansion of (nominal) national income. Contrary to the classical conceptions of business cycle policy, the government does not compensate the economic fluctuations but rather causes cycles of its own.

This macro-interdependence between economy and polity has been empirically supported for various advanced industrial countries, in particular for the United Kingdom, the United States and the Federal Republic of Germany. Politico-economic models are a necessary development of econometric models which so far have been restricted to the economy. Moreover they practically demonstrate the possibility of combining two thus far disjoint social sciences with the help of a uniform theoretical approach and a statistical method of research (multiple regression analysis and simultaneous estimation techniques).

The new political economy is only in its infancy; empirical testing of overall politico-economic models is incomplete and may be extended in various directions.

(1) Additional politico-economic relationships must be analysed. An increasingly important connection between economy and polity is the great number of enterprises that are neither purely private nor purely public but are situated somewhere in between.
(2) Additional decision-makers important in the area of economic policy, such as the central bank, must be introduced. The public sector should be modelled in greater detail by taking account of the federal structure and various types of governmental units.
(3) New aspects should be stressed, such as the political economy of international relations and the special problems of authoritarian and dictatorial governments in developing countries.

It should not, however, be the goal to extend politico-economic models further and further. The quality of a social science model does not necessarily rise with its size. For each type of question there should be an adequate theoretical abstraction that captures the problems considered as well as possible; other aspects may be disregarded in order to increase clarity.

The new political economy should above all be used to *improve economic and social policy*. The notion of a 'benevolent dictator', who maximises social welfare and therefore needs only be advised to that effect by experts, is mistaken, but it still dominates economic theory and practical political discussion. It is still possible to make economic and social interventions but they must be applied at different points and must use different instruments. The idea that economic policy can attain everything if only it is applied in an intelligent way (a view that has particularly been nurtured by the theory of quantitative economic policy) has proved to be an illusion. The normative propositions derived from traditional economic theory are rarely applied in reality because they do not take into account the interests of institutions, groups and individuals participating in the social process. An economic and a social policy built upon the new political economy starts from the mutual interdependence of economy and polity and, therefore, sees less possibility of influencing the course of society by outside interference. It can, however, apply its normative propositions more successfully because it works not *against* but rather *in the interest of* economic and political decision-makers.

Index

164 *Index*